THE DAYS
OF THE
THREE DIMES

THE DAYS
OF THE
THREE DIMES

Dimems or Dimes

LARRY MIDDLEBROOKS SR.

iUniverse, Inc.
Bloomington

The Days Of the Three Dimes
Dimems or Dimes

iUniverse books may be ordered through booksellers or by contacting:

iUniverse
1663 Liberty Drive
Bloomington, IN 47403
www.iuniverse.com
1-800-Authors (1-800-288-4677)

ISBN: 978-1-4759-8305-0 (sc)
ISBN: 978-1-4759-8306-7 (ebk)

Printed in the United States of America

iUniverse rev. date: 03/19/2013

It is 11:20 PM at night on the last day of March; it being the 31ˢᵗ day or night as it will be seen in the future.

"Dimes" was not supposed to start out like this nor was it supposed to be this; and indeed it was to be SCI-FI!

With my outlandish imagination I probably could have made a pretty good hit or miss at it, but I knew deep down on the inside it would be more predominately "miss" than "hit"!

So here we go and I will just do what God has enabled me to do. And that is to "just write my heart."

The book *AT THE CRSS* is a finished product published and it is in a few hands so far, no big sales or anything like that, but I did not expect that! My job was done when the book became print ready!

You see, it was and is more important for people to see and read that writing than anything else! You may say "to know the truth is to be set free by the truth!" It seems that everyone knows about *AT THE CRSS* but only a handful of copies have been handed out; not sold, mind you, but given away as the crème de la crème of my heart . . . "you know, gifts!"

The oddity is everyone seems to know about "The Book" as it has come to be called even before they pick up a copy or read one; but you will understand the "whys and the wherefores" of this if you ever get a chance to read a copy!

Stop . . . hold it right there . . . this book is not about another Book! I want to tear away the trappings of flesh and expose the heart that lay there withal! "I need to talk it out; I need to hear myself say I hurt; I hurt a lot, and this is the reason or reasons why I hurt; then maybe this exposure will allow a pharmaceutical healing of so many cold and dark days locked away in this dark and wet closet I call life to shine with a fresh breath and a renewed spirit!" It's 12:01 midnight; time for bed. My wife just got into bed and I am alone in my room . . . alone! It's April 1st—April Fool's Day—and I do with all my heart believe this joke is on me. Good night "April Fool!"

Hell-"O". I mean Hello. It's 8:56 AM on April Fool's Day. I'm starting the day in the arms of fiendish quiet and destructive hate! Seems all the noise and news today is—and has been for a few decades now—about a man they want to read and rape and a Book they are afraid to read and are not opposed to raping! O well, such is *The Days of the Three Dimes.*

You know why I stuck and stayed in a marriage where there has been no nuptials for 15 years and not gone a courtin' for a piece of "moe pie"? Well, it's probably for the same reason that I have not found myself as and being a minister in the House of God for about 5 weeks now. This being some kind of abomination in the eyes of good Christians everywhere "and I know it; and I don't care!"

Dear Reader, I'm tired. Actually I'm exhausted. My body hurts and my brain is in a stew pot. My faith, though, has not faltered; although many will say it has!

Yea, people have their opinions and, just like "butts," everyone has one! Yet a butt is still a butt and there is always one around; you can be guaranteed to find one on just about any corner you turn.

Though I realize in this confession my problem—I'm a "dad-blasted" realist. That's right. And I guess this is being honest? What I see, "I see." What I smell, "I smell." What I hear, "I hear." What I know, "I know." Excuse me, "Butt" for all of the "I'll go along's" of this world, I just know when the sun is shining even with my eyes closed, for I can even then feel on my ole skin! Why should I then stand and ask anyone "Is the sun shining today?" just to keep from stepping on the ever-popular toes of "John 'Q' Public Opinion!"

Don't get me wrong . . . I'm not angry with my people or my society "that people being the excepted name of the 'Brother', the 'Soul Brother', the 'Negro', the 'Negroid', the oppressed and suppressed Black Man" living in a state of supposed freedom, floating in society of humanoids that cannot wait to make us all defunct, void, exempt, expendable, and non-existent! The same society that we bore on our backs in the very making of all we see and hold dear. Yes, they rode in upon our backs and we smiled, danced, laughed, got high, and had sex with our women before their eyes, created our children, and gave them more beasts to ride upon for future

2

generations while they see as no more than fools and chattel for their own personal use!

Blacks are more likely to survive over a death dealing situation than any single group in this society than any other. Yet we stand in poverty even until this day of new birth!

I'm a dirty-mouthed realist. I ride along the road in rural America and I see shacks falling down . . . I cry. I ride along the streets and avenues in city and inner city. I see old tenant houses with broken walls, cut glass, concrete slabs, torn up old rooming houses that house more roaches and rats and poisons in the form of escape mechanisms called "crack", "horse", "weed", "alcohol", "uppers", "downers"; sex for sell that the cops turn their heads away and somehow don't see while HIV, Aids, and every form of disease ravish our Black women and threaten the lives of our children and plot to end whole generations of Black men and women!

I'm sorry . . . I read somewhere that it is not socially acceptable by John "Q" Public to write about certain actualities; and this most likely will not be read either because as "we" all know, "we" just don't talk about "shit" like this!

Forgive me—I'm just keeping it real. This little taste of the "paltry" is not really the Black race; though when we really look, we see far too many of us living this squalor with no way out of it!

When Public looks, we look at our advances and how many ever go slow up the hill molasses accomplishments we have aspired to! We always look at our MS, PHO, BS, BA, the Associatives and the like. "Butt excuse me." Maybe I'm missing something in process of numerical values. It seems by the very numbers of our own Black population there is an offset when it comes to the number of Black to the number of college degreed that we have to crow about!

Why then, who then said we are only supposed to write about or speak about that which is John "Q" Society acceptable?

It seems to me that we speak more about squalor in Africa and the Aids epidemic "than we have every modern convenience to overcome and conquer" right here not in our own backyards but in our front yards, highways, nursing homes, prisons, mental wards, and "high-rise ghettos? Yes, we do have high-rise ghettos. We speak more of what we don't know than what we do know and see every day of our lives!!

I'm not saying leave our sisters and brothers alone in Africa, but what I am saying is "let it be a unilateral movement from less to more for the

American Black as well as the African Black." A simultaneous movement to undo the genocide from the Sudan and Aids all over this country and around the world. We have the means, we have the money, we have the degrees, "thus the brains;" so what is the hold up? Are they waiting for us to just die off? Well maybe they are! We're certainly not doing a whole lot about it!!!

What I see "as a realist" is a cloud of euphoric bliss created by some phony accepted power that we dare not challenge. It seems that, as the song goes, we don't want to "rock the boat!" If I've got my bread and beans, why mess it up by asking why sisters and brothers don't have their bowl of beans and bread? This only chances the losing of all we've worked for and I'll be damned if I've worked all these years just to give it away to some damn body I don't even know! Why should I?

But what about the sisters and brothers that are working? My question is what about the millions of men, women, boys, and girls that are not working and not even enlightened by the media to let them even know they should work? Why in reality many of the millions of dollars and billions of dollars we represent goes to cover up campaigns to appease us so that we don't see the need to do anything, because we don't really see anything that needs to be done! We're used to getting in squalor, going through our day in squalor, going to bed in squalor each and every day because we don't see anything that we can do about it! This, my sisters and brothers, is the general consensus of our national and international condition—we just don't see what we can do about it!!?

Nothing bothers me more than to see a little Black boy or girl in a news flash of progress holding in their little black dusty hands, nose running, as they use their hands or a plastic spoon shoveling out of a plastic very colorful bowl gruel out of a communal pot that we have sent them! Wrong? No, it could be worse . . . a lot worse . . . but it could be a lot better . . . a whole lot better!! Why our kings and queens; why not some other? You don't know? Well then ask yourself why we sit and look at little boys having their feet chopped—and this is mercy—their brains blown out; their fathers' guts pulled out; the women raped, screaming and dragged away; the little children chained together like dogs; whole villages burned and ransacked, everything they know gone up in smoke in moments; and we sit and watch genocide like it is just "The Days of Our Lives" and nothing more!

4

This is Black on Black destruction! These men who do this call it ethnic "O God" cleansing! They are Black Moslamic Militia! Men with modern weaponry killing men and women who are Christian, who just happen to be Black as well and who are no more than simple farming people who try to scrape from the ground life for their wives and kids while we as Black men, women, boys, and girls degreed, agreed, and rich!! don't do a damn thing except wag our heads and count our dollars and go line check our bank accounts and stock quotes!!

Were you aware by the graph they flashed on the television the other day that Black people are now in second place to the Hispanic community as the race that contributes race-wise by capita to the overall economy than any other? And they are advancing further and faster than any other. They now are the ones to watch because they have more input into the American economy. And for this reason the whole society in America is geared to court the Hispanic dollar any way they can because dollar for dollar—"and everybody knows it's about the cheddar, baby, it's about the cheddar"—yes, dollar for dollar they mean more to this society than the Black man. Why? Because dollar for dollar, race-wise we are in second place as a money-producing people! Yet society still rides in on the back of the—(Can I use this? Let me think. This word to me is very caustic "butt" we say, so sweet!)—on the back of the Nigger! As it was . . . and if we don't get our shit together as it will always be! . . . it's because we are Black—not the color, not the race, not the society, but the place!

We're in this place and have been for far too long because we have the excuse that we have not been afforded the opportunities that everyone else has. People from all over the world come here and are rich already and have become a force to be reckoned with in ten damn years, and we have been here for at least a few hundred! I'm not laughing! I'm angry and I am tired. We have every on-the-surface opportunity . . . yes, I said on-the-surface. By census, it's all in place; yet by a functioning component—I'll write this again—by a functioning component, our opportunities really don't exist!

It's all a cloud of euphoric bliss only realized by a few, only measured by some, and seen by even less because the answer, my friend, is not only "a-blowin' in the wind," it is hidden within the binds of books that we still as a free and Black society are not even allowed to read because it has questionable content by other Blacks who are in position to only nod or shake their heads whether in public or private or just simply standing there in place. "Door men with PhD's, MA's, BA's, BS's, Associates, and the like"—people who have large amounts of money and, by the way, want to keep it at the expense of little boys and girls playing on broken glass laden streets and men and women who kiss with the women pressed against the walls in piss-stench dim-lighted hall walls, coming up big "pregnant" with the fellows laughing as she waddles down the street to the social services offices for food stamps because she for lack of "ed-mo-cation" has no job nor hope for one! Another lost branch of Zion!

Were you aware that the right race or the white race has the audacity to ask themselves this question: "Well, then why do they keep having babies?"

You know, on the surface I ask myself the same question. "Butt" being Black, it affords a reasonable, acceptable answer: You see, we—some of us—may have HIV and Aids, but so do many other nations. We just happen to be the sore-thumb on the hand of world society, so we are always seen first. Besides, we don't look like anyone else, or this is the accepted norm, believe it or not! Yup, we know better but get any other race up against the wall and the first thing they will call out: "You-a-Nigger" or "Nigger." It's as though Niggers don't have the rights afforded everyone else or am I trippin'?

But back to that great looming question . . . why do they keep having babies? Is it because they can't get enough sex? If that is the case, then why don't they use protection? Don't they know the welfare office gives it away free and so does Sister Sally Chiquita Royal Thompson Zully Jones . . . oops! There I go again; going against the accepted norm. Yet she does, and everyone on the block knows it!

Then it would appear that it is the Black woman's fault. Yet what about the Black girl who has the "swole" as it is called; properly the swollen eyes and the puffy bleeding lips and broken teeth, beaten, stomped, kicked, and bruised because she would not, did not, or could not open her legs for this intrusion on her only gift and wealth, the only thing she still has control over in her meager life, her own femininity! What happens to her source of joy and pride when she lays in a twisted, tormented, as well as broken heap while some big bold Black stud that all the girls chase after and just "luv" pulls his belt together after replacing it into his pants, putting away his "Johnson" and spouting off, "That'll teach your bitch ass. You don't stop nothin' do you hear? Nothin', bitch, nothin'!"?

This woman cowers on the bed trying to cover her only gift; trying to touch every hurt and hurting part of her tormented body and at last concedes and removes her hands to cover her ears for the words that pour forth from his mouth are far, far more painful!! At last her nudity means nothing . . . she is a broken vessel, another lost branch of Zion.

Yet why do they—the black man and woman—keep having babies? Why?

It's because out of all the hell the world gives and all of the hell, the bedlam, and the remorse we give each other that, that, Lord how mercy!

That little tender babe that lays there looking up into the eyes of this demon called society, stops "him"—"It—in it's damn tracks and for a moment that mighty machine is held still and cannot move by the tears so tender by this new born child. That no matter how the child got here is the hope and the promise lying on the very breast of a woman who is for, in that timeless moment, the greatest queen ever in life, "This Life", born!!

Now there in the "Box of Pandora" left!

Hope and a chance for a better and brighter day! For in each child there is the blood of some true king or queen; not the bloody hatred of a faltering Nigger that has already accepted his lot in life, who has his excuses for the way he lives feeding on the hopes of a nation!

Yet they are not the majority. Unfortunately, because they are not taught nor think they have to be, they have become the great minority; and we all stand in their shadow always trying to move away to a better town, a better time, a better place; always arriving with hope; and for a while all seems to be going well; just to have cold ice water dashed on our dreams in the great halls of knowledge and the hall of life that is afforded us, by a whispered word or a screamed word poured forth by a carload of beer drunken whites, "Nigger, Nigger!" This word that says you have not escaped nor will you ever. You're no better than your forefathers that we hanged; and still hang unbeknownst to the many of you right before your eyes and you are too stupid to do anything about it! Because quite frankly you don't even know that it has occurred and continues to happen, whether with word or rope, "Y'all hanged!"

It comes as no surprise to me that they would ask the question, "Why do they keep having babies?"

Well the reasons are many and varied. One reason is to offset those of us that you kill! Whether by putting into prison or mental wards; those that are lost on the streets, either killed by the police or killed in gangs or gang rivalry; or put away from the flow of life for life in our well-developed penal system which is primarily for the Black inmate who is there from teen years to old age and knows nothing else except survival any way you can—"dog eat dog!"

This is the flow . . . it's about staying alive. There are only by a few million more Blacks free (or so-called) than the thousands whose feet will never touch free soil ever again!

They lay and look up at there ceiling. They know every mark and indent, paint mark, every brush stroke that is there. After a while there seems to be forms and faces that take shape. And when they return to their cell, their eyes immediately go to that spot to seek for that form that they saw; and their comfort and their sorrow indeed it is truly still there!

You see, the imprints are a way for them by seconds to escape their world and condition. But truthfully, it is their torment as well because that freedom is also their reminder: "I'll never be free again! No, not ever!"

Sometimes even the harsh con will cry.

Yes, this being so we are taught that it is honor to serve this country in war. With commercials of the proud pressed military man who has now become the gladiator and the wall that affords freedom to every born American. Excuse me, except the Black. We have less as a people for the more that we do than any other major minority in this world!

Our men are killed and mutilated in war. They are accused of crimes they did not do nor know at military tribunals, and have even less of a chance at life because they were blackballed in the military for crimes they didn't commit. Yet we are the best fighting machines nature has ever produced; yet the anomaly exists we can't fight poverty, ignorance, violence, natural disease, and waste on our own strewn streets and our own homes, towns, and cities!

How do I know about the false accusations and the military tribunals that mark us for life? It's because not only am I a scribe, but I am ex-military. Busted for drugs that were planted on me, incarcerated, represented by a military advocate (given what I now know, didn't nor ever did exist) "The Vietnam Option."

This I was told gave me the right to stay in the service or leave at my own discretion with no more than a loss of stripes, maintaining a honorable discharge and all that it can afford a veteran!

Lock me up, take the stripes I've served for, accuse me of drug trafficking. "Ah, hello." Yup, I'm taking up my honorable discharge and yes going home! Goodbye and good luck! This is how I write . . . this is why I write. I know from experience what I am writing about!

Yet we are the American Hero; at least as long as you are in their ranks, as long as you don't question or buck the system. Just stay there, do as you are told, and don't get discharged. For as soon as you are, you become what you were!

Why do we keep having babies? Well it's because we keep getting killed and mutilated at home, overseas, nationally, and internationally. We as Black people are expendable!

The race most likely to have babies and by general consensus the most likely to fail!

Now we as a people know that these are all trumped up lies, but how do we prove it when we are only allowed to read or recognize what is socially acceptably for John "Q" Public?

There must be a common denominator that can set us apart from this mark of deception and degeneration. What is it about us as a people that this rides along with us—yes us—wherever we go?

Are we doing something or not doing anything to relieve us of our lot in society? Something is very, very wrong! Black people are more handsome and more beautiful than we have ever been in recent centuries. We are more sought after and intermingled, married, and birthed than ever. Why then this mark of failing?

We look and act like regular Americans, yet we don't have the same joys these people live; in and amongst them as we flow, it's like we are in this system yet not a part of it, even while they ride upon our backs to the future!

Forget about the whites or any other race. Let's just concentrate on each other. It's not like we don't have a voice because we do; but for some reason, without the expressed and effective, affective leader or leaders, we don't seem to have any power! Is this the reason that anyone who dares speak out with a loud voice is followed and watched, tormented and troubled even by the interior which is us ourselves—yes, we oust anyone of us who dares question! By us they are called fools, troublemakers, crazy men or women just because we know who we are and dare speak it with pride! Is this the reason we are watched—because we exhibit characteristics of leadership—which is demanded we prove ourselves and are threatened by others if we do?

Black people demand that you prove yourself to be a leader. If you show signs of leadership and oust anyone that will not step up to the plate, who refuses to be the whipping boy or leader for any people, who by now should understand the principle of "individual leadership," leading self wherever they find themselves alone are not! How can I say that we stick together? Yeah, right. And so do lemmings in their 7-year migration to the cliffs overlooking the sea to just dive in one behind the other to commit suicide and find death! It is said that by the hundreds of thousands they do this; but it all started with one leader, yes, showing the way to the sea then one jumping in to be followed by thousands more!

Yet it is also said that one simple lemming turns in these hoards right in that headlong rush to suicide; he turns and heads back in the direction they started and came. And believe or not believe, the rest turn with him and go back to whence they came and the race is saved. Now we as Black people are not furry little creatures called lemmings. But we do seem to have that leader syndrome. We don't do anything unless it is accepted by the entire race!

Yet every advancement that we crow about was enlisted or propagated by an individual who could not get the help of his fellow Black (or they did not believe in what he was doing or could not fathom what he or she was doing and, yes, were afraid to do what he or she was doing!) We only now in this modern era even know of the contributions Black men and women have given to this society and keep contributing right before our eyes; and we are not aware that they are doing it because the media does not openly make these kinds of accomplishments known, thereby leaving us standing where we have always stood—the "flunky", secretly known by many as the "whole" as a "fool!"

Whose fault is it? It's because when they see the Black, they see us dancing. Nothing wrong with dancing—it is a true power we possess! They see us singing. Nothing wrong with singing—it is the exhibition of our spirit! They see us playing sports—basketball, baseball, football, anything to do with ball. Nothing wrong with sports—this shows our gaming powers. Yet beyond these acclaims, the majority does not know that we have scientists, doctors, chemists, astronauts, inventors, economists, historians, anthropologists, adventurers, explorers, writers, police, FBI, CIA, teachers, bishops, priests, ship captains, airplane pilots, rocket scientists, biologists, surgeons, every form of health care workers, social scientists, librarians—what else can we do and do—yes, Blacks do that, too!

The sad part is that we as a people do not as a whole know these things about ourselves because many times it is hidden between the binds of a book! We even go to church and have to be bowled over by the Black with "knowledge" that we soon forget when the sermon is over; because we have the Bible lying on our coffee tables and we won't pick it up and read it for ourselves! It's no wonder these men in robes can tell us what they want and we don't question what they say; because they are our leaders and we lean on them for knowledge and understanding! The Bible even expounds, "My people die for lack of knowledge;" but it also says, "With all your getting, get understanding."

Dear, dear brother and sister: get some understanding and learn to lead yourself! Don't be afraid. Forget about popularity and seek knowledge, get yourself understanding. Don't stand and compare yours with someone else's; for what they show you may be for their own gain. No! Get your own. If it is a sound foundation, it is seen by all men and none can deny what they see. For the very life within them depends on the very self-evident truths, that we all who know hold so true! These are dividing factors that cannot be ignored or given away. For when you do, the very life and the stuff of life is lost; thus life itself. And if you want to live, you will accept these common denominators that rule the life of all that live and breathe!

Find out what is right—not a supposed right—and yes, apply it to your life. You will not be ignored. You cannot be ignored. You become the stuff of life. You become life. You become "Leader." You are leadership unto yourself. What are you? What have you become? You become strength—not what people accept, but what people, "the society," must have to continue as a people. Not just a people, though. You are the interlaced web substance that holds together all that is true and right, and the only thing that separates men from common animals led by instincts, not knowledge, dependent on their state of this or any other natural or cataclysmic event.

We have, as a people, been led to believe that if we "step" on our own, we won't (nor can we) survive without the whole. This has created an inbred fear over generations and decades of time that has been augmented by peer pressure which is supported, believe or not, by our hierarchies; which really support such actions for, in truth, their own survival!

Hierarchy "such is the church" which is and has become the focal point of this our society. Nothing wrong with that. "Butt" blind and unquestioning following creates blind leaders, who lead in turn "the blind follower" going no where in the last state confusion and extinction of the social order!

The question is who teaches self-annihilation?

After you have begun to be a self-leader, things will unfold like a well-formed "crepe" to turn over formed for the plate! As obvious to you as the warmth of a spring sun after a cold winter's eve, welcomed and enjoyed. "Understanding!"

This very society itself has instilled in its makeup, revamped over the generations to function as needed, an automatically self-actuating blockage, and if necessary a death to anyone that questions this system that we have been taught to believe in! This is the sham and the shame of this social order—this Grand Shit House we call America!

It hurts to sit and listen to these braggarts on cooking shows talking about what I'm writing at my table in what is supposed to be our home thousands at the very least hundreds of miles away; knowing that this and they will never, no never be questioned because of the seeming idiocy and madness of a so-called accusation of this magnitude. How can anything of this nature exist? The pain that truly exists is we are the last to know; and when they laugh me to scorn, they are really scorning and laughing at the whole race because we as a people looking right at the television cannot hear or perceive what they say!

The bold "Bitch of Babylon" rides in on the marked beast and no one even knows!

How can they know? They don't know they have been enslaved and freedom is a mere illusion . . . Paradise Lost!

As a people, the Blacks have been cheated forever and we will never be free because we are not allowed to think! We are not allowed to perceive on the same level as everyone else! I'm writing this and it will sound insane, and this is because we have been lead astray!

I pray to the God of my salvation that someone will believe this writ if no more than to investigate these goings on! Who will be wise as a serpent, quiet as a dove, as deadly as a fired well-placed bullet, and smart enough to use this newfound power without ending up in the loony bin for knowing that interactive television is now a reality? And when they seem to be talking to you—brother, they are!

I'm a realist. What I see, "I see." What I hear, "I hear." What I smell, "I smell." And what I know, "I know!" Believe me; it's not about me proving my sanity anymore, nor my proving that I am not insane. Either we are "chained" . . . and these chains—invisible and electronic—tell me you have not felt that something strange is going on and you just don't know what it is? Well, welcome to the 21ˢᵗ Century, Slave!!

What did I have the cahonies to say? That's right: "Slave." We are enslaved in a society that professes freedom for all people . . . well that is any people except the Black!

They don't even know that we talk to one another (at least as a whole) with no more than our minds because they don't allow them to know or to do this! At the very least, these people are servants and they don't even know it!

The Days of the Three Dimes has become a book of very, very scary truths.

You see, we have very Privy Blacks who know that many of our people who are committed to insane asylums have nothing, absolutely nothing wrong with them. They just have the unfortunate ability to hear the Beast and can't prove it. So they are locked away by the rules of this society and the ones that now stand by and say nothing, either out of fear of retribution or payment in the forms of promises or perks of which we can't question—"where did they get all of that from?" So they just keep quiet and the rest of us are suffered and laughed to scorn by the others who know what's going on!

What about the hierarchy? Well what do you think? Uh, what can I think?

You know the armed forces has to be by proxy if by no other means standing ready to send a wave over the Blacks that will make the genocide of the Sudan look like a Sunday Pic-nic! They created this issue and let it seep into our ranks a degree at a time so by the time we all realized it, the affect would be so far-reaching we would not have the slightest chance to overcome it! Yet if we riot, they will have the reason to kill us and imprison us for being militant and a very dangerous people, maybe even associated with the terrorists!

Believe it. They think we are snookered and have all escape routes blocked; and on first appearance, they do! But they don't know the secret that I incorporated into their precious system: I'm a Beast against Beast. Nothing have I seen in life that I loath more than this people: this civilization called the American Public.

I must admit at first I thought it was only a few prejudice bigots trying to have their way; and now I see it is the whole of the system. They have decided to enslave us even as we watch, and to set us free when they decide for their amusement. Ah! Excuse me! This is not acceptable. Not in the least bit to me. Not even for a moment of amusement at the expense of even one of our people. Not Black people not one. And the greatest peeve is to know that Black men, Black women, boys and girls are in on the very, very heinous joke makes me know that we have not advanced, not even one foot on the scale of survival than what we did when we first came here as chained and brutalized slaves from living in our own feces in the hull of slave ships! Excuse me! When in the hell did we forgive these monsters of pallid pureness? How can we sit by and watch them lock our brothers and sisters away in asylums to die there like common animals? When did it become acceptable? Who said it was all right and why?

Ah, Shit! This Nigger is crazy! These are the words you are using right now. But history will not be cheated and will hold up a banner for all to see to remember this "joke," this atrocity!

Even if everyone knew all but one, "to enslave, to mock even one is to spit in the eyes of every leader, every President, and every hanged man and raped woman that died getting you the right to plough your neighbor's calf!"

Don't you know when they tire of your jitter-bugging and showing white teeth in agreement, the next step for a people who have the most compelling emotion that they can devise, all you have done is to have postponed your execution? But execute they will! Welcome to the arena, Slave! Bring on the sweetest death we can find! Oh yes, let there be plenty of blood . . . you know how our viewers love "blood!"

Now I know that I may be jumping ahead a few decades, and you have no reason to doubt that these pale humans are kind and pure and nice. After all, they let us in on the secret and no one is suffering but one fool. "What does that hurt?" The fool should have known better! He thought he was smart. He didn't even know that we already heard everything and he was really the only "joke," a joke for everyone!

Yes, the immortal Black. How did we get here? Let's see. There were the race riots of the sixties and the high pressure water hoses, the dogs having at our flesh, and our blood flowing down the street in rivulets! Then there was the little girls burned alive in church, the Scottsburough boy lined up and down the street hanged by the neck on telephone poles!

Yes, Master. No, Master. And the blue story of the Blues Singer Bessie who died only blocks from the hospital would not and could not be admitted because she was Black!

We have prostituted our women, our daughters; our little boys have been subjected to pedophiles and outlandish hatred hidden by very clever people who would rather shed our blood than to eat when they are hungry; and they sit and poke fun at only "one" while they sell pots and pans on the television and we don't even know nor hear her, even know such a thing is even remotely possible. You got to give this white race a standing ovation. The greatest thinking Black mind in society either does not know of such activity, or they are too afraid of losing their precious lives or their status quo to even give us a fighting chance while they plan our extermination. Good men, good people who have our greatest at heart interest!

Those we depend on and yes believe in! They'll say in the end we were going to tell everyone but the time just wasn't right. Ha! Ha! It's a joke. Don't you see it's just a joke? Ha! Ha! Haaa! Yeah, a joke!

The Black man is the laughing stock of a nation and possibly the world and it's just a joke. That's all, just a joke. Why worry?

You know my guilt level is in the moderate range today. It's not high guilt or, hello, pain. It's just a memorial to all the highs and lows of this people that we obtained as we smoked our crack pipes, counted our money, or had the illustrious chance to have sex with one of the pure at heart, of which we found irresistible in the end of the conversation!

I'm not really being mean . . . I'm just meaning what I say!

Don't ya know we as a people have been playing at the game of Charades too long!

As a man, I'm disgusted with all of the blatant lies and the acts of piety for the sake of posterity while we lose our moral majority and tuck it away while we zip our pants and replace the bras upon naked breasts!

I'm sick, I tell, sick of knowing the truth and sick of the liars who call their lies the holy and righteous truth unchallenged because of their stance of piety!

Yet as a Black man, my tears sometimes fall still; and sometimes no matter how hard I try, the tears just won't fall! Waterless clouds carried overhead by heated and scorching winds—ya know, the wind of social change, the winds of indifference.

I seek as a "Black," a way to break these invisible chains; and then again I look around and everyone seems so happy. Then my guilt rises to conquer me and I know that I have looked upon her flesh. Lust did not depart, and I wonder is it important to be free? Do these people really know they are slaves and will freedom be welcomed?

I'm high now for lack of sleep and rest! It seems as though this pen has become an appendage and a part of my flesh, and you know this fight with my libido is truly unearthly. Why is it so important?

"Have you turned to Christ today?" is the question posed to me. My answer is hellish. Did you wipe yourself as you finished the last time you and her were together? Don't see me as your enemy—please! I'm your friend. She's your friend. We're all your friend. Sounds a little like "Mad House Walls" doesn't it?

Can't you see I'm looking for a little nod that says yes, I did it, and yes, I understand and I really would like to help but I can't? That's all, just a little nod! Nothing more.

This little "nod" would give me the desire and the apportioned authority to go about seeking away out of this blind alley this conundrum we've allowed ourselves to learn to enjoy with great rapid communication, this "contagion," this black magic and joy in our consternation we find our grand anticlimax; thus giving rise to our addiction, and over and over we pedal our wares with no apology!

Still let me culminate in the search and rescue effort of my people!

The pen, the pen, the pen went empty and I was sore afraid. I had to hurry and get yet another like a vampire hungry for blood, my thirst is not to be appeased. Let me alone while I drink in each word that I write.

It's fatback they crave, and it's fatback they despise depending on who you are! You are the self will of a nation; and that will chained and the impact great or small we must be free!

The immutable freedom fought for by our ancestors, insured by the Constitution, died for "by God" and we trade it for the impaction of our understanding, lost people on the last mile of the way! We have imparted our souls to this imbroglio; this, this confused mass, this acutely painful and embarrassing misunderstanding that we "embevrer" soaking ourselves and drenching ourselves; "bibere" we drink this blood!

I'm on it and I know it—on this "lunatic fringe." This is what happens to people who deem their right to become the luminary for a people who like to hide away in their blackness!

In my "lupulus" state I growl and sometimes I whimper just to sink my fangs in this luscious flesh of a flailing society! So good it is!!

People believe that I have some fiendish "misoneism" of this new order, "butt" it's just that I didn't know it was good. I always assumed that things misanthropic were unacceptable by the many. Nevertheless, as "Negrophile" I don't support slavery whether it is a neoimpressionism or not.

This book is now a true phantasm, but it's really a "Judas Tree" of experience grown throughout eternity—"just another one, please!"—as the Black is "marked down" each day!

How do we escape this bodice of such expensive perfumed, and espirit essence of feminine virtue? An unlikely enemy, wouldn't you say?

Since they know of our every movement and since they know of our "give over," it's wise to rationalize that we can't move freely and we can't plot our way out. We then must sit on Mamma's knee and learn to read again! And when we can, the "Hemlock" or maybe "Verbain"—what do you think?

Sing sweet lullabies while he's watching us on television and talking to us when he is pleased and for the—ah?—Luciferous Black that guard and watch, "O come magnify the Lord with!" Yes, this is the way . . . right up Main Street, Baby, "Just like they did us!"

Rome wasn't built in one day and America didn't die over night. It took time and much planning, a lot of agreement, especially from our religious leaders. How long I can't say, "butt" I do know Rome wasn't built in a day!!

"Naked Naivety" were one people; "Naked pumping butts ready for it," "ready for the fall" with minimal kicking and screaming they went along quietly! Do we agree, "question?" All in favor, give the "eye;" all against, "nay." No nays? The eyes have it and when they are cast upon you, "stand!"

Yet in truth we can't stand this and we need to run—Run, Nigger, run! But to where? Is there a place? A hiding place? We used to say we can find a hiding place in "Jesus;" now look around. Ask yourself, "Where's your faith? Where is Jesus now?"

Do you still believe, huh? Do ya? Do you still believe?

Is our sense, our morale still based in our religious beliefs?

Come on! Ain't nobody reading but you! Do ya? Have ya ever?

I have. I have a whole lot! Did you? Tell the truth—I think you have if you just would admit!

It felt good, didn't it? Just you and your own senses?

Yes, it was good. I admit and whatcha gonna do about it?

"O my God!" I just admitted it! I admitted that I did it!

How ya do it? Was your mind on Jesus all the time or did ya take your mind off him some time? How did it feel when you thought, "I just need a few minutes by myself?"

Yea, and you took it; you took those few moments. We all did. Why do you feel so guilty now?

Your guilt meter must be in the high range today.

<end excerpting>

"Hmm, interesting." It's not that you don't love Jesus, now is it? It's just that we needed . . . Ah!!?

You "pitch black devil." You set us up. You're the reason that we did it! It's your fault. It's your fault! You're the reason that we praised Jesus and we prayed to him and we sang hymns of praise to him! Every Sunday, every Sunday I went to church and you can't blame me 'cause I went to church and I know it! I know it, damn it, I know it. I went to church and I know it!!

Now this may be the very ravings we can expect to hear on Judgment Call, on Judgment Day! "Maybe, huh?"

I wrote all of this seemingly disjointed raving; but it has its place and it has a definite reasoning in that over the hot coals of traverse through this civilization Black men and women, boys and girls had and have to walk barefoot alone! Though through agony we still survive. Yes, the Black is the most likely to survive a death-dealing blow; more likely than any other race of people.

Long story short, we are the survivors and I don't mean the program, at least not the one on the tele.

Besides, we really can't trust the "tele" anymore or anyhow. If you wanted to mass program a people, how would you do it? What is the most pervasive conveyance to all in the society?

Were you aware that Blacks that live like third-world people in shacks with tin roofs have television many more times than you can find food in the same house?

Say for sake of argument that you just wanted to program a people to ensure that they stay in their place and offer no defiance in and to your culture, what medium would you use?

Smoke signals, maybe, word of mouth, the rising of the sun, and the going down of the same!

Maybe you could pay them with goodwill perks or lovely little get together conventions, radio, telegraph, telephone, tell a woman, satellite, or sexual frenzy . . . what about threats on your life? You know, you can see that the most valuable medium is the very media itself, encased in an electronic and atomic field that we don't see nor feel.

The Jews lived, worked, loved, laughed, played, sang, went to church and to their death by the millions in the presence and by the hands of the Nazis who in truth showed no sign of what they were preparing to do to those pitiful Jews, not one sign! It was a rehearsal act right in the midst of them and they knew nothing! Not one damn thing! Nothing!

How did the Nazis accomplish such a horrendous deed with the whole world looking on?

The sweep was quiet, quick, and organized in such a way until the Jews went gambling along all happy and at peace, not believing, knowing that the German Nazis had their best, yes, interest at heart! It was all for their welfare that they were loaded into boxcars and carried away to death camps for extermination, and they did not for the most part even ask why! Yet if they did ask, it was for their protection and they believed the hierarchy and they died because they did!!

Germany was very much in those days like America is today! You say, "Yeah, but Hitler was a crazy!" Boy what a copout! Don't you realize that Hitler drove no bulldozer, dug no death trench, poured no gas, shot no Jew . . . the people did! Hitler was mad with power, his people were crazy. The Jews were helpless sheep. Even the great Jewish minds had no recourse, no place to hide, and indeed they were dissolved first!

America is high on power. The people are acting out crazy deeds. They practice guerilla warfare in the mountains. They use real bullets, real guns, real bows, real arrows, and they let real blood!

Our President is crazy. He loves war. He hates Blacks. I don't care what he says—it's what he does not say! When did any American Prez let an atrocity like the Sudan go on without sending some kind of aid?

Do you have any idea what these beasts do each and every day while you scratch and chaff and wallow in your supposed freedom? People get ready—there's a train a-comin', comin' for to carry your dead ass home! You better wake up. These people that we walk with, talk with, eat with, and work with are planning something against us because they desire a pure race of people, a pure society—they are tired of Niggers!

In the great high towers of wealth and industry, they'll meet in the restroom. Here's the conversation: "How's Sam coming along? Oh, he's all right; he don't know nothin'. Does he suspect? Naw, he's deaf. Ha, ha, ha! And blind, too. Yeah, they all are! I can't wait! Me either!" Sam comes in . . . "Oh, hey Sam. You're doing great work! Yeah man, keep it up! Yeah, you'll get your reward!" Sam just laughs . . . . sooo happy he's a part now. He's big business corporate; he lives and rubs elbows with blue chip stock! Sam says, "Man, I'm lucky!"

But just let a Black call for aid and that same white man shakes his head NO!

This is the conversation between Black Sam and Black Jim, the impoverished: "Hey Jim, how ya doin' man? Oh all right, I guess. Did you check on that for me? Oh yeah, Jim, but your score was too low and you know you had a few marks on your credit report. We'd like to help you but we can't. I'd help you if I could. My hands are tied." (He really means his hands are chained.) Sam boldens up and tries to force down the greatest disappointment, a "NO" he has received from a brother that had promised him that he would help!

"Chaquitha, can you come into my office? Yes, Mr. Kilroy, I'll be right there!" Into the office she twists and closes the door behind her and giggles while raising her skirt! "Girl, you my favorite." "I know it, Joe. Come here, let me see what you got for Mama, you naughty boy!" "How's Chaquitha coming?" "Well and all the time!"

Don't you see our boat has come in and we're happy! Why rock the boat? I don't understand what he wants?

"Sarah what are you doing? Nigga, can't you see I'm waiting in this damn line like I always do? You know how the Welfare is! You might have to wait, 'butt' it's free!"

Yes, Sarah, free and chained to the Black social worker who sits on her high perch behind the desk, who slams a clipboard in your face, and growls out to your face, "Fill out the whole form or we won't help you!" Page after page you sit there writing, trying to answer questions you don't many times understand and afraid to approach the counter anymore because of that Black Beast of a social worker that sits there with your babies' lives in hand, knowing that all she has to do is to take your forms and go back into the room while telling you take your seat and wait "Slave." "You wait until I say 'come.'" And you know that when she says "come," you better hurry up to that desk ready to do whatever you are told. You know what the sad part is? After all that writing and turning to your neighboring poor person and asking them the questions you are afraid to ask the social worker, this wardened servant to her fellowman, who sees so many come through that door poor with their hands empty and held out for help, the same woman is as black as you are, has surmised in her pebble-sized brain that you are trying to pull some trick to keep from working! She knows you wouldn't raise your skirt and didn't get the job and want! Yet she can sit there on her high perch looking down on you like an owl about to feed on a mouse and have the audacity to look you square in the eye and as much as you need help say, "NO, we can't help you! But, but, ain't y'all supposed to help people? I said, 'NO!'" This word rings off the interior of your skull like a bomb, and the hunger pangs don't hurt as much as the stinging tears you are trying to hold back. Will ya come now? Of course, you will!

The end result: "I'll do any thing you say! Do you promise? He-he! Yes, yes, I'll promise. It's not so bad. We'll have food from these callous bastards!"

Who are we to question why ours is to do or die?

Prejudice, paranoid, degenerate, hateful, crazy Black Devil you! We don't like you! You're bad business and we don't believe anything you say. We hate you! You, you dirty fool! If you had any sense, you'd go on somewhere. Nobody wants to hear what you're talking about. Nobody!

Let's look at the real problem here, and it is complexity at its very core.

First of all, many people that go to the Welfare office are from nowadays third and fifth generation Welfare survivors, and it is a chain. Not only is it a chain, but it is a chain of events linked ever so intricately one link to the other!

The first level is seated in the education. At least that is what we are led to see and believe! You see, many of these suffering saints are uneducated! They are young, many of them, and still have a chance to get an education. On the other hand, the owl that sits behind the counter is educated and wise, but has lost the heart and love connection with his or her people. Now in her eyes, there is nothing wrong with this. "I worked hard and went to school. I got mine. Why in the hell can't you get yours?" "Secret" hatred for self!

Funny thing is she started out on the road because she really wanted to help people, especially her own kind!

Now there is formed a unilateral positioning—the haves and the never will have who love the have nots! I'm not crying . . . at least not yet!

The first generation have nots were the same people as the Blacks who now have!

Then where did this division take place? I'm a realist and I don't really believe in luck; somebody bit the bullet way back when and then there were those that got shot with the bullet way back when. Oh yeah, some were lynched, some were imprisoned for crimes they did not do and died in prison, some were locked away in mental institutions, and some became lab rats—well-fed and fat! Yes, and some left home, some became drug addicts, given drugs by their peers who taught "it's about the cheddar, baby, the chedda'!" and fed our young, strong and healthy Black young men this opposing poison! Some lived for a while and some went from corner to corner seeking money and having sex and producing babies that had no connection to their patriarch of the line and family lineage!

Why did they leave home? Good question; glad you asked! Many of them were (back in the early hundreds) left to grovel anything they could from the ground, and their only pleasure was to lay naked beside their mate and wives which ended in the joy that only the pleasure of sex can bring—tired and sweaty aching muscles after a hard day's work that began at 3 AM in the morning in Mr. Smith's field where you worked and then you would move to your field where you share cropped for part of the tobacco or food you produced there and the rest went to Mr. Smith because he let you have a piece of ground to work as your own!

Mama after about a month would come smiling to the door to hit you in your aching mind, which is always trying to figure a way to feed your nine children and your wife, and she says, "Sam, you still got that ole crib in the barn?" He looks up confused, saddened, happy, and in joy! He grabs her and kisses her face all over because baby makes ten! "I wonder," he says to himself, "if it will be a boy? If it is, he can increase the crop. Well, at least in a few years. But baby has to grow up! Through cholera, dank cold nights, pain and torment, baby has to be—just has to no matter what—he must grow and he must be strong. He must!"

As we advanced as a people, so did our chance at success; but this always depended on the men risking their lives in the coal mines or the steel mills, making big money—forty dollars a week and board because they had to leave home to work. Most had no education and had to leave home early in life! This was the beginning of the concision for the Black man and his wife who was left at home to take in clothes and ironing. If she was lucky, she could work on her knees polishing Ms. Sue's hardwood floors all the day long! This was good work and my ladies would some receive old clothes Ms. Sue would give them to wear! Bless God, thank you Jesus, just a taste, but a taste that posed the question: How could I get my own clothes like this?

The Black man away from home and away from his wife sometimes was dragged to the clubs of the day by the more experienced veterans of life. Men who for a long time lived a double agenda: having a favorite woman in the clubs that offered them very special favors for part of their hard-earned money, whiskey, drugs to get high—and, by the way, this is how we first became addicted to the feeling. But were you aware that drugs were introduced to the girls, as they were called? These girls who passed sex for money and sometimes disease as well, carried back home to the country and transmitted to the wives who had no idea why they could not get the stank off themselves, not knowing they needed a doctor and his care; many of them dying that could have been saved, totally ignorant of their condition or even how they became that way. The odd thing is, there are many such women even today! I must move on . . .

How, where did these drugs come from? They were not grown in American fields, not in an abundance, not then! But the drugs were imported by white men that owned ships and docks and warehouses and dock workers. The Black dapper club owner ran the clubs and with an iron fist, club and bullet! But when the till was counted, the money was given to the owner who lived uptown. The same man that owned the steel mills owned the clubs, the dapper Black, the girls, the drugs, and the lives of Black men, women, boys and girls all over America.

If you kept your mouth shut, you could make the cheddar, even if you did eventually completely leave your wife and your children for "Lilly," her drugs and her Ahphrodisins that heighten your desire and hook you to her satin perfumed bed.

This, this the beginning of the concision working in the Black family!

The woman left at home to fend for her children would accept the fact that Charlie wanted more than just to be kind and visit. After all, he was a goodly man and a preacher; and he would even give her a piece of money at times. That wasn't too bad until one night he comes by and asks for the impossible because she is married. But he doesn't seem to care as he backs her into a corner in his house and begins to tear at her clothes. She can't scream and her muffled screams go unheard!

He does what he wants. She knows she can't tell. This is the 1918's. She's a woman. She knows she has no one to turn to because they will blame her and mark her and her children!

He comes by anytime he wants now and she doesn't cry or scream. She just whimpers like a beaten child! Another concision in the Black family and the church leader is the father of it! Even looking, they dare not tell!!

It's not so bad. He gives her a little money. Her flower, her dove is starting to show signs of womanhood and he is always trying to get her to sit on his lap! One night she hears screams of torment from the next room, but she cannot move. Yet she is a mom. She rushes in with fist and arms flailing at his naked body. He just knocks her away, maddened in his lust!

She doesn't know that the poker is in her hand. She doesn't count the times she strikes his head. He just lays on the bed in pouring blood! Oh my God, the preacher! She stands quivering with her daughter in her arms, both crying in shame, pain, fear, and torment! Where is her husband? Drunk and filthy lying in "Lil's" bed and she can't stand the sight of him!

The trial was quick and the children are left alone after the hanging. The oldest child looking on the limp, dead body of her mom, the only one to care or ever will again! The kids are taken in by the foster home. Some went to fairly good homes and believe or not got, yes I said it, a good education; some became indentured servants in homes that were supposed to provide a family life; some slaved in sweat shops making and sewing clothes for nothing more than food and a bed out of the rain.

Then there were those that ran away and ended up in these very special clubs, some cleaning spittoons and mopping up puke off of the floor; some were noticed in the club by the white owners and were called to their back room offices to be raped and beaten day after day!!

Those that lived became very good whores and were glad of it—besides the money was good and they had the finest food. If they used drugs, and most ended that way, a home, and you were considered a lady! The boys didn't always fare as well and usually died early in life, either by violence or violent whites who despised any Nigger who professed to be human! These families in the beginning were not broken by the family leaders but by the pressures placed on the family by its society for self-preservation. They left home, yes, but they left in order to feed the mouths of the ones they loved, lured by the stench of the almighty dollar.

The fall did not take place in and of itself by self-motivation, but they were led astray by other Blacks who enjoyed the fast life and the lure of money, drugs, liquor, and sex that was provided by the women who found this living an alternative to pain and hunger, begging in the streets!

Yet none of this could have transpired without a root for growth and a source of nourishment for growth.

The Blacks in the beginning had no money; this fuel is the food that fires our social machine!

We didn't own the paper mills that made the paper to make the money; we didn't own the presses that printed the money; and we didn't own the finished product that bought the ships that ran the trains that carried the whiskey, the drugs, the women!!

We were just the backs that this society rode in on!

I spoke of lab rats. This is not a caustic throw off on the Blacks who have progressed, but it is a direct hit at Blacks who seem to have forgotten where they came from—hold their heads up in the rain and look down their noses at less fortunate Blacks as if they have no value!

It's more than a coincidence that we have highly educated Blacks and high yellow women; it appears that in the beginning the two were synonymous. Later, although by hook or crook, the so-called "darky" (by the avenue of war) went abroad and found a world of freedom that he could believe was real! He could walk where he wanted and sit when he or she pleased. It was a "dream!"

The Black, despite common bigoted belief, is by no means a fool! Quite the contrary. If given the slightest chance, his mind will grasp any concept and he or she will expand the idea to its highest level of logical conclusion!

This is the major factor in the creation of the road houses and bars and dark rooms where you could get it on with a high yellow woman, the closest thing to white!

This kind of woman was sought by men of all races and as a bonus you could get your "high" on! Now it seems on the surface rather innocent and business like—"everybody did it." But the shame of it all, they're still doing it "in the name of business and enterprise." And any enterprising Black who just happens to have no conscious could couple with a moneyed white man who was also enterprising and needed an up-front flunky.

Working together they could mire and block the minds of the other Black men who, unlike the world traveler, never knew that freedom of any other kind even existed!

Now this served two purposes. It kept the servant a servant and, for lack of education, the "slave" a slave while exciting the economy at the expense of the Black man's blood!

Where are you leading us to? It's quite simple. This is the explanation why it appears that Black men are ignorant, right in the face of Black culture. Because until the most recent years—say after World War II—the educated Blacks in America had no way or did not deem it correct "believe it or not" to teach their fellow Blacks what they knew!

Don't know why, but here in the millennium we can find this atrocious activity still rearing its ugly head: "The Blacks have gotten on the bandwagon again!"

The bold sign boards express on the televisions, magazines, newspapers, computers, radio, and such something called "the haves and the have nots!"

Which are you? If you had to think about it, you are Middle America; but if you are Black, you're probably in the—"excuse me"—in the welfare line or not many feet from it! And we have lost that pride that says, "I will not forsake my brother . . . the hell with you!" "Haves" we will continue to survive; we will forsake one another! It is not a question. It's about religion. It's not church. It's not about one or one million of us having Aids!

It has nothing to do with the fact that this society has murdered each one of our leaders in succession because you know what? I am an individual leader unto myself. "I can lead myself!" I don't feel no way tired. And I don't need anyone Black, white, blue, Jew or Gentile to tell me it's all right for me to think! This is not the Middle Ages! I don't need anyone to come along and tell me this. I already know it for myself! I am no one's fool!

The world has changed; but for the Black man, it is essentially the same. Example: Have you driven along a highway and each mile looks so fresh and clean, have you? Did by chance you see a large high fence all along da' road? Most people don't pay it any mind as they whiz by. They don't think nor do they have the time to know what is on the other side of da' fence! Goal is accomplished. No one has to know! And out of sight, out of mind! And out of the hands of the "Chamber of Commerce!"

Do you know they spend more money keeping that fence up than they spend on the "potholes and pitfalls" in the Black Community?!

Why? Because behind that Grand Fence is the largest and the smelliest and germiest trash heap that God ever allowed on the face of the earth!

I bet you wonder why your children stay sick. Just to take a wild guess . . . I would say that the run off and the gases from that trash heap go right back into the water system even though it is purified and into the air that we breathe every day of our lives! The fence is pretty ain't it? I said, "da' fence is pretty, ain't it?"

Guess what? Here's a tear jerker. The insightful me has come up with a "new fence." It's called "burbs" or suburbs. Now here's how it works. It's called "City Planning" where few Blacks are in on when it's being planned, if any. You got Ghetto Land and outskirts of town. (These two are about the same thing!) So over the years, by and through enough argument, a housing development is created; and they take a few Blacks out of Ghetto Land by the process of HUD development. And they move a few into these on the outside reasonable nice homes. "Nothing wrong with that."

But did I tell you, you have to "qualify?" Most Blacks, believe it or not, don't qualify, even with the new laws that say they must qualify! Now here is the conundrum: somebody must live in these new dwellings! For some odd reason or another, poor—"excuse the express" because I'm poor too—poor whites, Hispanic, and other races do qualify! The law says that in the positions—that is the work or professional that govern "who's in" and "who's not in"—the government says that these positions must have a proper quotient of minority workers! Like the Black woman that sits on the high stool looking very much like an owl that is hawking a rat for dinner and knowing your condition shakes her head and says "NO!!" and walks away, you standing there with one baby in your arms and two babies, one at each side, and knowing that you have no husband!

The process is the same as the fence guarding the trash heap! Yet now we have a fence within a fence! One fence is those new spacious, modern facilities for people trying to, and desiring to, stand up! The other fence that is closest to the moneyed people and "haves" and government, the "always had," run by people that just happen to be "us" who have to make a quota!

This quota absolutely must be filled or the little money from the "haves" and the "always had" will be "cut" or stopped altogether. And then those fine homes will start every time to go into disrepair. The fence closest to "Ghetto Land," and guess who gets the blame? Of course it's the ones behind the fence! I'm not calling us trash—God forbid—but it is a fence!

We respect ourselves and we do the best we can with what we have to work with. And I love you, whether you believe it or not, "God loves you too!"

We just have to recognize fences!!

Now I'm going to hit you hard. Got to get you breathing again. Got to get your heart pumping. Gotta keep you alive so you can keep yourself alive, so you can keep somebody else alive!

We create our own damn fences—especially in Ghetto Land—and we blame the law!

"We are the law!" We are the people of the United States of America, and to the Republic for which it stands, one nation under God, indivisible, with liberty and justice for all . . . you know the rest! We are the law!!

Without our backs to ride in on, this Republic would die!

Use your power; use the law; learn everything you can about the law! Make the soft seats in Congress and the Senate "hot seats" in the Congress and the Senate! Get pissed off! Do what they never expect you to do! "Take the bruise." They will bruise your head anyhow!

Build up your money reserves buy farm land. Put people at your back that can be called at a moment's notice on every level of government. Then vote derogatory and wait it out for a few years, knowing already what they will do.

The next time that comes for you to vote, vote positively. Make them beg for your vote. Make them put themselves in such a position until they have to answer to the law or go to jail or go to hell!

The ballot for 2008 has to be the apex for our social climbing and status quo power positioning in all time as American citizens! The standouts for presidential campaign gambling are a true potpourri of ethnic and economic straight-face poker players with a myriad of accepted and rejected morals and stories of delicious "White House" ribaldry not unlike the days of that Nixon era! Yet very close to a story of the "Bobbitt." No, I did not say "Hobbit;" although entertaining, in those no one was laughing, but the blood could be seen to flow.

You may ask, "How did I get here?" This may be taking a great chance, but I take this chance not because I am Black; but I am a Black that is for all its value 56 years old, born in some of the hardest times an era can throw at a people!

I am not only Black, but I am also Cherokee. I find my blackness leads the assault against oppression, suppression, and insults that this society directs for dark skin people!

My great-grandmother, bless her heart, is gone but not forgotten. A Cherokee by birth, yet when she married Joe Bly in her 16th year and him being 19 years old, an "Iron Foundry" worker, and having his own home worth in the thirties $1000, by standards a rich man! But what made Pa-Pa rich was not his standing nor his marriage, because by Ma-Ma marrying, she became in the eyes of the standing law a "Negress," but she stood by Pa-Pa and gave him 13 children, 12 of which were female and one boy. The records—that is the Census—shows Ma-Ma as a Negro, but she is Cherokee! Is this important? Yes, because of your association in those and these days, you can truthfully lose by law your birth right!

Is this important? Yes! Man's law has successfully overcome the natural process of God's creation by a mere pen stroke. I searched the records, and I cried happy to find my heritage and saddened to know the limits that this society has taken and gone to belittle a people!

Now where is he going with this? I lived through social oppression and suppression, but I recognized more of it because Pa-Pa and Ma-Ma were the great wall around their children and their offspring. That same wall stood against all corners in this society and was fortified and emboldened as well as energized by love and mutual respect that will, could, and never shall be overcome!

Now this brings me to one of my points. It seems that in the up and coming year we will elect the highest official in the land; that is the office of the President.

For the first I believe ever in my lifetime we have a serious contender for the seat. I say we, this being the "Black!" Yes, he definitely is someone to deal with. I won't use any names; everyone knows to whom I refer! Will I vote for him? Well, that's none of your business. This is still a free and democratic society no matter how much slander and drama, as well as outright lies and dirty laundry it can produce! We still have the vote for who we damn well please! Don't forget this. We didn't have by supposition. It's because of people like Pa-Pa and Ma-Ma who refused to give up what they believed in and what they lived knowing full well the consequences of their actions!

Now let's get to the meat, the very jest of this conversation. It seems that it's still very important to see us marching down the street singing "We shall overcome," and to acquaint any Black with this modern operation who is in a position of authority!

How did I come to this point? I lived through the segregationalist era—we as the people walking hand in hand, clutched side by side, was the way the Black exemplified the solidarity of a nation known as the "Negro!"

Great move used with great expertise and a needful show of family, which for such a long time we had no way to identify with. "Movin' on up," yes, we did. "Good times," there are a few. "All in the family," sometimes. Yet somehow as usual this society that rides in on our backs has figured a way to even turn these definite junctures of advanced supremacy in a dwarfing society better known for its kicking the crutch out from under the man with one leg and shooting the blind man's dog, has again started a very, very seditious and sublime campaign to undermine the efforts of the "Black!"

How? The process that we have used to reward ourselves and the—"excuse me"—"get over the hump." If they can bend us, and they will try, be—excuse the words, nothing vulgar intended—be yes, "humping us!"

If they can show this contender as a "we shall overcome" prospect, they can then prove that he is just another . . . and move on!

But this man shown sometimes as holding hands man to man and brother to brother is not just another . . . !

He need not disconnect himself from the Black race. Because if he does, two things will happen: He will be accused by us as a flunky for this white man not having our needs and conditions at the forefront of his thoughts. Number two, if he does not consider being Black, the Black will not consider him being Black!

This being true, "he must" realize that this is not 1967; this is 2007. The problems are the same for the Black man, Black woman, Black child, that is; but society is liken to the crouching bear waiting to feed! We still need solidarity; but as the "Day of the Three Dimes" impart, we also need "expressed individual leadership" showing this nation that no matter where we stand together, holding hands or separate and alone, we are necessarily leaders unto ourselves; whether one or a billion we rise, we rise to every occasion, and we stand for right, though right has not been afforded us!

What if the President is a Black man? I submit that we will have a leader that is not unaccustomed to the penalty of the injustice that law can rear in the lives of every man led by the custom of prejudice.

This being said, I believe with all my heart that any man understanding the onslaught that penalizes all people with nature will seek to correct the foundation that is cracking and threatening to topple the building of democracy.

This in itself will foundationalize a better world! Am I prejudice? Yes! Prejudice against any and all structures that threaten "human!"

Why do I write this particular segment in these "Dimes?" It's because I saw a picture with Blacks holding hands, side by side, and I knew that because this society has not advanced in a reality, "and I don't care what the commercials emphasize." As Blacks we are still driving Mercedes and Jaguars, riding in Rolls Royce and Limos, but they lay their eyes on a Black like "Bessie" only blocks from the hospital we lay and bleed and die because skin is black! Don't believe me. Take anyone of us out of that car, that status symbol, and catch us in a questionable circumstance. They will still slam you against the wall and the sidewalk letting you know that you are still living in 1951 and you are still "A Nigger!"

"The import" let this Black man show his solidarity with this people and let this Black do what he does best—lead any and all people as a man of no distinguishing marks, except strength of character, purpose, will, desire for a better world for all men so that we can springboard out of the 50's into the new millennium as leaders and teachers; but more importantly, look beyond his skin. Stop trying to connect him with only the, yes, "Negroid Race" because of his identity and see him as a "human" and a "man" who just happens to be a great leader of all men!

It's possible, you know. But how will we ever know unless we see beyond the fearful hand holding Negro of the sixties? And, yes, we were fearful and we had a reason to be fearful because many of us were killed because of it, even in a modern democratic society, yes, where freedom was for everyone but the "Black!"

See us holding hands? "Yea," but unafraid. The threats have not relinquished themselves nor the very real chance of death! We have still horror invoking people in this society. But let them see us holding hands. And let there be no mistake—we hold hands as a memorial not a crutch to great women and men whose shoulders we stand upon!

Why did I say women first? Well now, there seems to be on this April the 11th day of 2007 a gripe.

It seems that a renowned radio and TV commentator has taken a direct swat at some of our grandest college athletic scholars and women, who just by chance happen to be, by majority, Black women! The comments by all consideration were racist and anti-feminist in nature. This man carries a great rapport with the national white majority because of his standing and his falling of people who listen by majority to his commentary!

He's had his hand slapped and, yes, he has apologized and I would suppose that he was suffering from temporary insanity endured by subliminal ingredients of hundreds of years of accepted misgivings about Black women and no small degree of well-guarded and protected ideals which are and can be found throughout this race! Oh, they're losing it slowly?

But when a man can by his mere words (that's why I'm so careful) influence the very outcome and thought patterns of the society that he lives, which by chance is already "top heavy" because of comments against a people and a particular "sex," it would appear that his obligation to the society would take on a greater value and substance and not be so shallow and bind the hands and feet of the Nubian because of the texture of her hair and the shade of her skin; not in any which considering the content of her mind nor the intent of character nor the depth of her spirit, let alone her sweet and gentle femininity!

It would appear that I am attacking this man . . . but is he any different than the previous predators or predecessors who think like this?

This man is getting up in age and he knows the many roles that the Black has played in these United States of America. He also knows—it's no secret—of her advancing movement and accomplishments here and around the world. But like an aging boxer—"com-on coach, I can take um; com-on coach, just give me a chance."

You see, when the grammar goes, we reach for straws. But it is no longer acceptable to use "my women" as chattels for anyone's advancement!

This poor man may be ruined, but he is not ruined by what we did but by what he believed! He said "the Rappers" and the content and context in which they hold the Black Nubian, and the way they spear and sing about them was the real spark that seduced his belligerent blubbering in relationship to these scholars who have never shaken a tail feather on a video! And indeed are the next leaders and shakers for this troubled society!

Now let's give everyone equal time. "What about these rappers?"

I have lived, I have danced, I have laughed, and I have wondered about these "women" trying to be kind and honest. Of rap, it is a high value industry, driven forward by "the rush" . . . I'll say it again, "the rush!" In the old days, "the rush" was acquainted with the heat and thrill and ecstatic joy that the heroin user invoked when he stuck his needle into his main vein and pumped the bulb full of liquid heroin into his vein that would "rush" directly to his heart and brain! I don't know myself. I never tried it. But the joy of it was so great that many heroin users became instantly sexually excited and high beyond compare. Many of them (as I write I feel ashamed) would claw at their genitals, drool running down on their chest, and drift away to some land of euphoria—"lost men and women!" Yet as I said earlier, these Blacks . . . and not only Blacks, but many races, but particularly Blacks . . . had not the money in the beginning to buy ships or boats or mule packs to get this trash onto these shores! Guess who did. Not many Black people own ships, not even today. This said, ultimately who do we blame?

"Rap" is a rush! It is an acceptable rush accepted by society, driven by money. Exemplified by all things that men seek for to excite and fortify their lives. "It's a business!"

Many of these women who work in this industry are black, but not exclusively. And there are quite a few who would be the common prostitute if it were not for this acceptable way to earn a living! Not all these women are uneducated; some have degrees. But it is the lure of the Almighty Dollar that beckons them on this journey to create the rush for a sort of society of people who need more and more of a high that they can have—inclusive to all races—but not having to worry about going to jail for! Supply and demand! You demand; we supply. If the need wasn't there, the business wouldn't exist.

If Rap is anything and the pretending (for the better part "Rap Ho's") and that's just what they are—"actresses" putting on a show for a needy society that wants to express its most ancient and expressed carnal desire—the Rappers would be out of business!

Yes our nation, "Babylon, the Great Ho!"

Now make some sense of it. These women have chosen their profession—and profession it is, however viewed—but as in years past, "Shirley Chisom" chose not to relinquish her seat on a bus to a white man and was jailed for it!

Yet as we all know, the dives and houses of prostitution were quite often visited by white men who preferred the company of Black women for sex and entertainment. This was their way of surviving—putting on shows and acting. But they were not Shirley Chisom! What are you saying, Mister? Well, there is a dividing line and we need to recognize it!

Some Black women dance for a living; some Black women are actresses; some Black women are moms. Black women are as diverse in their survival tactics as they are to their beneficial input into this sorry society. We need to stop lumping them all into the same ball of plastick!

Frankly, I can see clearly now and I know if one thing is common to all Black women, it is a profound determination to survive!

But let's not confuse the Ho. Even though her services on the many varying levels is just as needed . . . and she is not alone, because Ho's come in all levels . . . even though in many cases this is her chosen profession . . . and let's take a quick gander at reality. The woman actress acting like a Ho may have a college degree and have taken dancing as a profession and in truth is just that—an actress and not by any means a whore.

Yet when we look at them as men—and we all do, if it's just a glance because they do look good and tweak some part of our male libido which gives rise to their success and their great demand of which they supply.

These women are not the Shirley Chisom's of the world. But you try to step on one of them and you will find yourself face to face with every level of woman born!

Now you must understand that our women, for the greater part, are not acting. No! They are very, very serious about changing this sordid world for all people, especially for their sisters who pretend to be Ho's and who are Ho's, so they won't have to be Ho's no mo'!

Men of all races know what you are looking at and not what you suppose it to be!

Reverse your thinking. They are first queens, Nubian intellect, wise beyond centuries. Then watch them and don't make, but watch. And if by chance they prove to be Ho's, then try to return them to the status of queens and Nubian intellectuals. If they are actresses, let them act.

Yet always—and I repeat, always—respect because your mom and your sister, your aunt, your grandma; from time immortal brought us to where we are and we owe them that much for their suffering for this society called "Black!"

Now we as Black men are trying to springboard. Brothers, we can't springboard by holding our women in a state of double agenda. If we are going to climb, it's not going to be with Black women at our feet! It's by necessity that they be by our sides! I tell you, if you can lead, it's nothing better than the Black respect! Yet remember our women came from queens. And I don't mean from Queens, New York! If you are going to be weak, and if you continue to be strong and succor off of her strength, she will rise . . . she will rise and she will stand and the queen she was meant and born to be, and she will be!

We as men, yes, as Black men even in the industry of music must and I'll say again, "we must" hold our women to the level of the highest esteem. And when they are acting, we need to let the public know that acting is part of the industry. And what you all do in the bedroom is private so that the public does not low-rate the Black woman and lump them all into the same group. Let's make sure they see their beauty, but be sure that they don't forget the profundity of their minds!

Sometimes the only way to resolve a long-lasting "need" is to search that "need" and question its position in your own "person."

There is no woman that I honor or respect more than my own Black women. Yet if one of these women were to exhibit themselves on one of those hip-hop strong beat "hot beating hearts" videos, I would look and yes look hard to see all that I could see!

The question to my person is that one of those wrongs that I argue against to my fellow Black man; is that going against the Black woman and is that disrespecting her femininity or is that just part of needing to know more of her?

Question to my person—when did watching her shake her booty that we love so well less than going on the web and checking out the spam that offers us a greater view of the woman we need to aspire toward raising to a height of glory they so much desire and deserve, when have we forgotten or did we just put our "high fluttin" ideals on the shelf because they are just good lookin' and good to look at?

These are just questions I'm asking my "person." You see, I've crossed that border and let my eyes roam a little too! No, I'll take that back . . . "a lot!"

Yet I've long since caged myself in my house and do not go out and just use my sister, my mother, call them everything but a child of God and move on! All right, "self," what are you really doing? You know that band-aid can last for only a while and then you will have to face reality again!

Yes, it will only last for a while, but I'm not allowed to sponsor my scar because when my trivial world comes up against the mountain tops and valleys of the "Blue Ridge," and I hear screams of fear, rage, and abject torment springing from the open and gaping mouths of babes that knew no fear!

When the sky sprinkles sugar dusting snowflakes on a people that cannot understand nor explain their pain, their anguish, or their fear!

When the routine that has never changed for generations on that university campus called Virginia Tech is splain by screaming and running horrified feet . . . across the television screen there are more emergency vehicles and special tactic units, police cars, men in uniform, guns, rifles, protective vests, helmets, and visions of a nightmare in this what was and is a historical day unlike anything ever dreamed or imagined!

I sit and scribe what has become a dilemma. You say a dilemma? Yes, a dilemma. This word is mundane and completely useless as many words that were used on that day and shall be used in days and years to come! No one, no one will ever be able to define on paper or photos nor anything else the rank horror that was felt by the hearts of every individual on the day of "Massacre!"

The day when the whole country was put on standstill and the world looked down on a tiny college town called Blacksburg, Virginia; and stood hand-to-hand, shoulder-to-shoulder in the grip of sorrow, fear, amazement, anguish, and grief! Many families not even knowing if they were even allowed to take a breath; realizing at last, not selfishly but as joy wrapped its arms around them that were spared the horror of those fateful words. How do you tell a mom—black, white, brown, Jew or Gentile—that the child you carried for nine long hard months, the child you watched grow up and make you the proudest parent in the world, the one that went away with part of your heart in "that suitcase" . . . how can you say, "We love you; we love you so damn much and we can never stop loving you! Never! Never! Never!"

This is a page that I have no control over! Maybe they are trying to tell us that, "they love us too!"

I won't write a number because these young people are not just a number in a history book! They were diversified; as different in their own ways as each star is in the sky! As unique as their choice of study; as individual as their heartbeats! They can't nor ever will be a number. We don't see them except in our minds, hearts, spirits, and souls. Yet the student as the teacher can never die nor will ever die as long as we as a human society live. We are their "life;" trust, we are their memory. And when we light the eternal flame that will burn, someday everyone that sees it for as long as that great hall stands it will be a memorial to "Virginia Tech Hokies" and their indomitable spirit that cannot be extinguished nor will be extinguished but will burn even brighter on this earth and have a witness in the heavens every time we look up we will see "Hokie Pride!" Each time a distinguished graduate walks that walk of a "completed study," when they hold that parchment that says this one is for you! This is a symbol not only for Virginia Tech, but for all of what we have forgotten this country to be. This is still America. We are still all Americans. And no matter what country we hail from, we all seek the freedom that only America can purvey! We are the only game in town. We are the only star in an ink black sky. We are the anchor that holds within the vale. We have the right and the ability to make a choice and to choose our course; and we had better not . . . better not . . . relinquish it for any cause to anyone or anything!

This freedom is the same reason that by the hundreds of thousands Americans of every race have fallen on the battlefields and in the streets of this free society called the U.S.A. and the United States . . . not the divided states, but the United States of America!

Now our people fall in a place that is supposed to be a safe haven and we reel; but we have not fallen. Satan has shot a volley and we reel; but we have not fallen. Not a volley nor a million, billion volleys, no man, no beast will do what they try so hard to do . . . "America will not fall!"

Where and what went wrong? I see us hurrying along destined to keep our appointments that we may accomplish our goals. But if we are to survive, it will be in the same harness pulling in the same direction. Two horses in a harness cannot plow a furrow if each horse is pulling in different and separate and self-appointed directions. We must all pull together! The common cause for the common good; that we may have and find the perfect ends by using the same means!

Who knows, maybe if someone had dug a little deeper into the mind of the assailant, maybe if someone would have just seen his shaken and distraught and his disturbed mind, if we could have just slowed down enough . . . !

What I do know is it's time and it's past time for America to wake up . . . wakeee uppp!

How many wake-up calls do we need before we begin to understand that we have strayed from the path that our forefathers set for us to follow? Don't become brass-browed and stiff-necked because of this tragedy. Don't hurl toward heaven, "God, where were you? Why did you let this happen?" and turn your backs on the only door left that we can enter and find the balm that can and will soothe our aching hearts, "Satan has power too!"

When this kind of horror occurs, remember that in the order of heaven and earth and, yes, even hell, there is a time and place for all things . . . yes, all things. Just remember, God has not forsaken this world nor will He ever. When we wail, His heart is torn and He has a place for that beast called the devil, the one that tears our babies and bleeds whole nations to death!

Remember we view a nation that suffers what we suffered in one day "every day; everyday!" This nation we are trying to protect has been suffering this horror for decades and hundreds of years. Does it make it less painful and is it less important when a baby dies in Darfur and where so-called aids victims have no value? "Why are you saying such things, scribe?" Because if we don't look around and see where we as humanity stand in this world of men, we will be standing in their world . . . and we are!

Poetess, dear poetess, I am a fledging poet, proud that the words that gave us and Virginia Tech a shot of raw courage and immaculate hope; words that entered into not only the students and faculty and onlookers; words that infused into the very meat and spirit of every American in this world, no matter where we stood on that day . . . "We are Virginia Tech . . . We are Virginia Tech!" Those words to the living that they could continue on, not fail, never give up, never quit; these words fell from the lips, pen, mind, heart, spirit, and soul of a "Black woman!"

No matter how we as Black men view you, Black women . . . no matter how some of our men try to pretend "Black woman," we will always view you (looking up) you are God-awful wonderful!

On this day, that day, every day, I think that Virginia Tech is the cornucopia of American pride! "Go Hokies!" Go!

It's hard to write on the original plane in which I started because of the great deluge of information that is pouring in every day about the horror that transpired on the Tech campus. Somehow it does not seem fair to write anything else but things concerning the plight of us all, especially the ones closest to those who are now no longer bound by the things of earth! Yet writing a book of any kind takes courage as well as not a small amount of diversity, even when times call for a spearhead assault on a particular subject.

Knowing this and knowing of the wounds of each one involved here in this part of the world, the emotional and mental as well as spiritual disfigurement of all of us caused by an individual known by name and ethnic root, an individual who will stand shoulder to shoulder with other names such as Frederick Davidson, Gang Lu, Charles Whitmer, Edward

Allaway, and now Cho Seung-Hui—all hateful and monstrous people who will lie remembered by the history books and not forgotten as some of our most distraught and destructive of all our humankind allowed to walk amongst us living!

The one real and very valuable truth, though, this is true, is that the ones we know as the "innocent fallen" will have their place in history as well!

Being human in this world so filled with unidentifiable homo-sapiens, men and women, that we cannot predict or be anymore sure of than "the beast" that walks amongst us all, we would expect to be dissected and segregated from that power that "steals, kills, and destroys;" yet we can't for "Satan is very real" and works amongst us all!

We can't see the good without seeing the cruel, the bad, and yes the very, very evil! Thus when history recalls our loss, we will see them all—the good and the bad!

The trouble we have is that we as emotional creatures have a great need to get back at the ones who have hurt us so awfully bad. Coupled with this is the looming question in all of our minds—no matter your ethnic background, at times this dark cry is a mute of "why" hurled at heaven and into the very teeth of God—why did you let this happen to my and our babies?

The first point is hateful and just plain wrong to the ones left behind. Why? Because out of all the ones lost, there is just one, only one, to punish for these heinous crimes against man and men. Not an army we have to battle, to fight—win, lose or draw—just one in all the cases except a very few the act was carried out by just one very disillusioned, misguided, misdirected, or very ill human being! A question arises here, "How can I call such a brut a human being?"

The answer—out of all the animals that walk this earth, only one, and I mean only one, will rage and have within his or her capacity to carry out or have the desire sick or well to crush those of their "own kind" with such ferocity and blood lust madness; "man" the intellectual and intelligent beast and no other can nor will!

Inject: "Earth Day" is upon us. A time when we celebrate the Mother of us all! A time to stop and regroup. A time to take a serious look at the way we as men are destroying the only planet that we know of that can sustain our unique type of life form. It's also a time to look at how we as men have subsequently went out methodically destroying this very same earth that we need so much for life!

Ultimately we must take a very cautious but honest look at who we are and what we do in relationship to this world and to each other.

It is no longer a comfort to expound on "I am this race from this country" and act out the segregationalist attitude that "you are that race from that country!" No, we do not have the convenience to rely on our prejudices as men that we may bolster our pride!

There is no pride to cling to when the world we live on is dying and our fellow men are too!

Second point: Our need for justice unrealized; that fist shaking, cantering noise, trying to banter with God about His seeming lack of love or care about us or in truth our loved ones.

Now I move into this paragraph on very shaky legs because of the newness of the wounds. I want to be very tender and I want to handle that problem as diplomatically as possible.

Yet I know the truth can only be told one way, and that is as the truth! Truth is God has not forsaken us. And with every moan, every earth shaking cry that fell from the lips of those torn who feel that they can never nor do they ever want to heal, for fear that if they heal they will somehow be cheating the one last recognition. If this being so, then we will hold onto pain in this heart that bleeds ever so much!

Although this being ever so true again, God has not forsaken us; and indeed His arm is not shortened that He may not bless. Quite the contrary. He heard our cries; He sees our pain; and like any good father, He cries with us!

This then brings up a myriad of very hurt, bitter, and needful questions that we need answered, and we need an answer right away—not tomorrow, not some day—God, we need you right now! Where are you and most of all, although we don't see them, we need to know "Where are our loved ones?"

I'm sitting here writing these words and simultaneously realizing that I can't act as "JAH's advocate!" He's just too big, too powerful, and too wondrous for me to explain, let alone protect!

Yet I can say from experience this one thing—no matter how horrible the situation for the hour, "God is love!"

This statement in this hour of trial may take on the assuming role by the manipulation of the "beast," as ludicrous to the minds of all that live to see what has transpired; but that is what the "beast" does! He creates havoc, horror, and pain then transfers the act and the guilt somewhere else; yes, and to anyone else but "self!"

"Liar" is too a mundane of a descriptive name for the beast! His eloquence in manipulative history writing and social waltzing around and in issues that he has created can only be topped by God's words of "Let there be!" This being true, it is not hard to see him baiting mankind with unanswerable havoc and seeing him pointing directly to the throne of God for reproach!

Again the question: If God is so omnipotent, so omniscient, so very omnipresent, then why doesn't He just crush Satan and stop him from doing these horrible acts of atrocious behavior?

If we ask this question, then we stand as judge and place ourselves in the position of God and reduce ourselves to the level of the beast, ultimately carrying out the very desires he intended us in the first place!

God did not and has not forsaken us, and in order for us to even begin to fathom this through the grey mist of our fears, we need to begin to realize the state that we stand in as human beings! "It appointed once for man to die; then the Judgment!" Man's earthly existence is oh so truthfully temporal and is not on this side of "Chilly Jordan" eternal, and we must die! Not one, but all.

To scribe any kind of definition of the above statement will, can, and shall place me in a very precarious position as the pen of this writing because I want to ease pain and promote healing! This process will make me into a monster of sorts or an opinionated, heartless advocate of JAH's; and this in itself is a bad position to find one's self when all and all people at this point want to forget the pain and suffering and need truthfully to heal!

Yet also true is that there are many who really cannot just accept that those loved so much are just gone! There are those and maybe many of those who need comfort . . . no, not just comfort. They need a foundation to rest fears and cares upon! Not myth, not hope, but a truth that they can count on beyond anything ever known or felt in life. And it begins with the question: Is there anyone who can tell us where they are now? What happens now? Can you give us hope?

This country, and I mean these United States of America, has a foundation and I, not as some self-appointed expert but as one who is 56 years old, through trial and error has found one concept to lean on and point to down through the years as unyielding and never yet to be found in error. This is our foundation of faith! Never mind your position on this believing or not believing—the precepts stay the same. This country is based on some very sound doctrine, and this being our trust in some higher power! Be it what you may, we do (even as atheists) feel somewhere deep down that there may be some power greater than us!

All of that waltzing out of the way, I can conquer fear, hate, sorrow, pain, anguish, and this terror, too, right where it lay, right in the heart of the matter. Let's strike the one and leave him that is at fault with the One that can and does make the difference, settling once and for all our cry—where and why?

Our forefathers believed. Let us take solace in their belief, shed the much-needed tears and once and for all know! No, not the knowing of "I hope" or "I guess"—but beyond anything else I do know and have no doubt in this one thing: that my loved ones have a comfort and a comforter!

How do I know? Who am I to say? Who made me so damn smart? I know the same way our forefathers knew!

(The death that redeems:)

The holy writ says it this way in Hebrews, Chapter 9, Verse 15: "And for this cause."

What cause? What cause? That cause no greater and no less, "our loved ones!"

For this cause He (Jesus) is the mediator, the go between, the advocate, the lawyer, the mediator of the New Testament that by means of death . . . who's death? . . . His own!

That by means of death for the redemption, "the saving" of the transgressions that were under the first testament. That testament was death. Without saving grace, all were lost; but by the New Testament, they which are called might receive the promise of eternal inheritance.

Verse 16: "For where a testament is, there must also of necessity be the death of the testator."

Verse 17: "For a testament is of force after men are dead: otherwise it is of no strength at all while the testator liveth."

Then the question arises—who's "will" was it and to whom did it belong?

The answer is Jesus, the one and only Christ!

Verse 22: "And most of all, things are by the law purged with blood for without shedding of blood is no remission."

Bare with me. "Christ, the sufficient sacrifice."

Verse 23: "It was therefore necessary that the patterns of things in heaven should be purified with these, but the heavenly things themselves with better sacrifices than these."

These being the blood of "bulls and goats!"

Verse 24: "For Christ is not entered into the holy place made with hands which are the figures of the true, but into heaven itself, now to appear in the presence of God for us."

Yes, us and your loved ones . . . our loved ones.

Verse 25: "Nor yet that he should offer himself often as the High Priest entereth into the holy place each year with the blood of others,"

Verse 26: "For then must he often have suffered since the foundation of the world: but now once in the end of the world hath he appeared to put away sin by the sacrifice of himself."

<end excerpting>

You may say I don't understand all of that mumbo-jumbo; but as we believe sin entered into the world by one man's mistake, we are then all to inherit the penalty for that sin; that penalty being "death."

Yet God, the author and the finisher of our faith, loved us so much, so very much, that even His own judgment could not set freely in His heart for the ones He created, the ones He loves; yes, even His own children. And God not being able to lie, for the lie He would tell would eliminate all, made Him give all that He had for all that He made; that all being "Christ," His Spirit first and that of men the flesh in one, that "Christ!"

The same, the testator of the new "will!"

The inescapable: We hate to look at this one point, but it is the very foundation of all we suffer and all we believe or disbelieve!

It's the one thing we spend more time trying to elude or ignore than all other points in life. It's the one reason why many of us don't go to the House of Prayer in our life times and end there whether for our friends' going home ceremonies or our own! It is summed up in this verse alone:

Verse 27: "And it is appointed unto men once to die, but after the judgment . . ."

This "to die stuff" is in itself, believe it or not, an acceptable premise; but this is not the whole spectrum! It's that Judgment that incurs, and this is where we find ourselves with our lost loved ones! Where are they? How are they? Is there more to life than just this horror show called "life" itself?

If there is, there are a lot of people who really, really need to know!

We need hope, and on this day it's not for us so much—although this is inclusive—but how are our loved ones?

An answer. No, the answer in this—Hebrews, Chapter 10, Verse 19: "Having therefore, brethren, boldness to enter into the holiest by the blood of Jesus,"

Verse 20: "By a new and living way, which he hath consecrated for us through the veil, that is to say the flesh,"

Verse 21: "And having a high priest over the house of God,"

(Not just any priest, but our priest, the priest for mankind!)

Verse 22: "Let us draw near with a true heart in full assurance . . ."

Let me say that one more time, just in case you missed this very important point . . . "draw near in full assurance

". . . of faith, having our hearts sprinkled from evil conscience and our bodies washed with pure water."

Verse 23: "Let us hold fast the professions of our faith without wavering."

For He is faithful "Jesus" that promised.

This same faith as the faith of our forefathers that founded this great nation with the help of all men—Black, white, Jew, and Gentile—none being the less!

Verse 24: "And let us consider one another to provoke unto love and to good works."

<end excerpting>

Not this maniacal screeching and wall-eyed behavior that is so prevalent these days, as I see upon the streets of this city and many more like it; to go as if it were a private feast and do this instead; after all it's easy to hate but it's hard to love the one's we hate. Yet these are the credentials necessary to claim these promises procured by the death and blood of Jesus, the Christ, and not make the death of our loved ones non-exempt and without purpose! By acting out prejudicial hate, are we any less than this latest "tormented" Cho Seung-Hui? Are we any less than the author and finisher of this, that one Lucifer, Satan, that Devil? Then . . .

Verse 25: "Not forsaking the assembling of ourselves together as the manner of some, but exhorting one another: and so much the more, as ye see the day approaching."

<end excerpting>

What day? The day . . . the day of the time of our end also! "For it is appointed once for all men to die, then the judgment."

The Bible says not to make your decision "until you have heard the end of the conversation." This being an end, let us know how and where our loved ones! It is already fixed in the heavens: "They rest!"

We are truly the ones we need to consider and that before the end of the conversation; before we take our last step; before we take our last breath. God has done more than His share. The rest is up to us! Hate or not hate. Love or not love. "Choose!"

The Dimes was never supposed to walk, sit, or run in this direction. And I need to say at this point that I am not a novelist. But *The Days of the Three Dimes* by any other name most likely will be called a novel, at least of sorts. This being said, I have come to realize that those of you who are really novelists do have a legitimate statement when you say, "Novels have the tendency to take on a mind and spirit of their own. And many times we are just swept along with pen in hand at the novel's every whim, trying ever so hard to manage the reins of this thriving beast!"

Now if this paper that has the audacity to call itself a novel will allow me, I will try to write its "will" again!

If I remember correctly, I was lain and splain on the canvas of life and my heart was open to some very invigorating concepts that displayed our women as honorably as possible for the time and space allowed!

This pursuit, if I will admit it, laying no little honor on the penmanship of the writer, and admit it I must because to say less is a left-handed swipe at a beautiful people and a woman by the greatest majority left in the downward flow of life's upward climb—yes, I mean "flushed!"

I never meant for this lady of culture to end this way for this is not the way she began. "How do you know so much, scribe?"

My simple answer is I was dared by one of the most self-perfected females, having absolutely nothing in total control of her world . . . and I could go poetic on you and say flowers sprang forth where she stood! You might say this guy has gone overboard and no Black woman ever exuded that kind of prominence; although I have lived into my 56 years on this earth and I can still remember seeing a hardened rosebud bloom in her hand with the stem between her ring finger and middle right before my little amazed and awe-inspired eyes!

It then would not be an oversight to say that as for this woman—my great aunt, who happened to be half-African and fifty percent Cherokee—that flowers did bloom where she stood!

O great novel, where are you taking me? Where are we sailing to now?

I have the reins, yet I am afraid to use them for one of the base lessons that old half-breed taught me was in a story of a very rich white woman who lived on a plantation . . . and in those days women wore very elaborate "dress" for riding. On this particular day a "fancy" (as I like to call them) came out to the exercise yard and she being very foppish in attitude and dress announced that she wanted a very high spirited animal to ride . . . no, I do not mean a Black man.

This little trite statement being said, maybe the novel will let me continue.

She pointed to the animal she wanted and the keeper, being Black and slave but too very familiar with the horses, told her the horse had not been properly broken. Being the "fancy" she was, she insisted, "Boy, bring me the horse; bring me the horse right now and saddle it!"

Now at this point my aging aunt began to laugh in just that way a Black woman laughs when she knows—excuse the thought—"the jig is up!" Pun? Well, maybe just a little one!

The boy put the bit in the horse's mouth with no little effort, the colt fighting at every move! "Missy, are yo sho yo wanna ride dis hoss?"

"Boy, put a saddle on that horse!" By this time my little sister finds herself laughing too, of course, not knowing why. Maybe it was the old Negro dialect my aunt used to describe the boy! "Yessam, yessam, right away," was his answer as he saddled the horse.

Now women that rode in those days rode with one leg around the horn on the stirrup called "side saddle," this being the style of the day. Ladies didn't straddle a horse; it was un-lady-like and "dash" or shameful.

Yep, she was determined to ride that horse not knowing the first thing about riding any body's horse. She was dressed for it . . . had on the right kind of hat, just right petticoat, just right riding shoes . . . and she was white. And the boy (which was a man) was Black. And how could he possibly know more than she about horses?

"Help me up," she warns in that just so persnickety manner. "Give me your hands!" The poor Black man clasped his fingers together and made a step for her to hoist herself up and on the animal. Yep, on the animal and then it was on . . . or should I say it was "not on!"

Hum? She was on the horse. She was kicking the horse. She was saying to the horse, "Giddy up, giddy up, move! So you heard me, move!" But the horse just stood there.

My aunt stopped laughing long enough as she told the tale to inject, "Y'all hush," as we were laughing so hard, not even knowing! "Y'all hush," she said again, trying to stop laughing herself!

"Sometimes it's not so important getting on the horse, as it is knowing what to do when you get up there."

I wish my aunt could have been around to tell old George that after he had been in office for a while. Even though he is from Texas, sometimes we need just a tad more common sense people to inject the old hypo in just the right spot, "If you know what I mean!"

She just sit there rocking back and forth, whipping the horse with the reins and hollering, "Giddy up, giddy up!" Finally the old Black man could take it no more and screamed, "Missy, pull back on the reins and it will go!" "What?" "Pull back on the reins!"

Missy got the idea and pulled "hard" back on the reins!

"And they're off!"—Missy and the young colt! The horse picks up speed. Missy starts to scream, pulling back harder and harder on the reins! That ole Black man just stands there looking as off they went at a full gallop! Missy's hat flew off her beautiful curls fixed just so for the ride; her dress was flying up in her face, petticoat for the whole world to see; and she's pulling back harder and harder on those ole straps hollering, "Stop! Stop!" By this point in the story, my sister, Aunt Mary, and I are rolling as I can see plainly that this was not the smartest white woman in the world. And when Aunt Mary explained her petticoat, I died . . . I died!

The "boy" as she called him was running after them, more afraid for the young horse than he was for Missy! "Missy, Missy, turn loose the reins; turn loose the reins!" She looking back, "You stop this horse. Do you hear me? You stop this horse right now!"

As much as I hate to ruin a perfectly good party, I just remembered that, like Missy, I have the reins of this thriving beast in my hands as well; at least the reins of this <u>Novel</u>. And like Miss Missy, I need to know what the heck I'm doing. And I'll prove my point!

Missy in the story I would guess about this time was about to wet her pantaloons. Aw! What the "flying sandwiched sardines" . . . she was pissing her pants! Now!

Somehow through her clouded mind of horror, the boy's words pricked her ears. "Turn loose the reins," is all he could say, standing there looking. The horse running and kicking up his hind legs, her holding on. By sheer luck or misfortune—however you want to look at it—she let loose the reins.

(Now this is my place in the sun.) Most horses are trained to slow down or stop by pulling back on the reins, but the thoroughbred in many cases is just the opposite. You pull back, they go faster. You relax the tension, they slow down.

As you guessed it, she turned loose the reins and dropped them altogether. But the joy of it is for all old Black women who tell tales to Black boys to teach them what it means to be men, and for every Black man and every slave that was ever called "boy," yup, she let go. Missy just let gooo! Right in front—and I lie not as the story is told—right in front of a big ole mud puddle. And this one is for all the smart asses and psychics and know-it-all's in this world . . . I can still see that dress, that same Black woman slave or servant that had spent a long night, many nights after working in the field, up around her butt slinging mud off her pearly hands, wiping her face, that made sure that you could not tell whether she was white or Black or whatever and at times like these in life, you know, "it don't matter!"

The only thing that didn't make me laugh is what my aunt didn't tell me; I guess I've always been perceptive!

I can still see some beautiful rotund Black woman with a rag tied around her head, or maybe some sapphron that took time out from duties with ole Ma's! Washing and bathing miss "Missy" as she bitched even more! Do you think a woman like that will ever learn to use the reins? I don't! Yet somehow I feel pride for holding tight . . . not too tight, not too loose. I believe I managed the reins of this thriving beast and have controlled the pen or the novel's spirit had mercy; and I have writ!!

A time has passed since I last fought with the spirit of this novel, and as I dropped the reins of this thriving beast, arose from my seat and lay down the pen, it seems time has slowed its onward march into the future, bringing with it the "ultimate," that being the end and the conclusion of another dream!

Though it does seem that time slowed, it in reality has passed quickly and it is approaching the end of May 2007. I needs move onward and upward as I sit; I rise to this occasion and this need.

I started in the beginning by saying "I did not know what to write or how to write it;" so I supposed "I would just write my heart!"

Thwarting all of the anxiety that comes with putting the ink into the paper, I strive with my emotions and again write my heart; which being the upper accent of my most adored being on this ole earth, that being in her multi-faceted posture "The Black Woman" and her son "The Black Man!"

I know a few things about many things and many things about a few; but every time I find myself exploring me, I find that I actually know very little about myself. And in order to write "Black," one must truly understand what that word epitomizes—all 5' 11½" of it! At least that's what it is in my case. Some may say and ask "Now that we know how high, how wide?"

Now you would think upon first exam that this is rambling or pure ambiguity, but just think about it. When they spoke of the "steel drivin' man," he was "so tall," "so wide," and his fists were "so huge!" Now when they speak of the plumber, his feet are "so big," his arms are "so long," his . . . well you get the idea!

It appears that whenever a Black was spoken of, it was and is always about his physique rarely his mental train! It's odd, but usually when we direct our conscious in reference to him and his mind, we almost always see a Black woman! I guess that's why she is almost always the sought after by every race of men. What did you say? I said, "That's why she is almost always the most sought after female in the world . . . sought after by every race of men!"

"Make your point, scribe!" Well let's go up and down, back and forth in time, not to linger too long in any one spot. If you want a woman of the evening, who can and will never turn you down or let you down? Who do you call? I'll give you a hint—it's not Ghost Busters, buster! I hate to say it and revel in it. At the same time, from time immortal, it's from the Queen in Solomon's Courts to the upstairs maid . . . from the student studying the newspaper at ole Ma's knees to the doctor of some whip-lashed Black in a freezing slave's dark and dank clay-packed floor of some freedom-seeking new African in his shackled and manacled cabin; fighting the new beast, a tawny lion that he rarely saw. It was the Black woman that taught us to first read the Bible, the free book for free men and slaves, but not the Black man because he (at this point in time) was not even considered to be human. And even the Bible—the "Word of God"—did not even apply to him! Not to get too far off the subject, but didn't Jesus the Christ die for all? Just an injection. "O yea, I forgot." Another thing (just as an injection of course), is this "forgetting thing . . ." I used to think I had a real problem until one day I caught this white dude I worked with—under his breath, is about the best way I can describe it—telling me to "forget." Yes, that's what I said, "telling me to forget what I had just supposedly learned!"

I guess some Black woman must have blessed me because just as my thoughts and memory were heading into that dark abyss of forgetfulness, I realized just what he had said and why I was truthfully "forgetting!" At that point I openly asked him, "What did you just say?" "Ah, shut up damn nigger" was his real, yea real reply! I said, "I'm not a damn nigger and if I were you, I wouldn't get in the habit of calling me one!"

It was on him telling what he could do and me bantering about what he could not do! It's a good thing we were friends, if you can call that some kind of friendship! I guess it was.

Back to my most adored species of feminine wiles . . . The Black Woman. She has never ceased to amaze me!

Just as "John Henry" was good with "his hammer," as a steel drivin' man—ha! They never considered the Pap's that gave suck to ole "John Henry." And at whose knees he had gathered his prowess and true strength! Yep, none other than his mother; who still unto now goes nameless through history. It seems that many a Black man can give, if he only would, the greatest honor to his alter gender—the female of our race!

Yet we can hear from the "speak easys" of old to the hip-hop of now the equating of our Queens with the female dog! Damn, how dumb does one get? Excuse the American modern Negroid English! "Damn, how dumb does one get?!"

"All right, scribe, you're up!" Why is it that you fight so hard trying not to give in to looking at that most voluptuous Black bottom that just women sport? Huh? Huh? Why is it that if you see a picture, hear one described, or go into some land of euphorical libido driven bliss that you can't leave it alone and always rise to the occasion? The answer may lie in the statement (driven by the heated and inflamed brain of every idiot that ever said it), "Man, look at that bitch!" We need a fraction of one inch taken of one appendage over all of our body, one at a time until each appendage is no longer there; then begin on another until we sit stupidly on a stump looking at the one extension of ourselves that drove us to the limits of idiocy in the first place. And have the most gorgeous drop-dead Black Nubian dressed in a low cut, pure white nurse's dress cut thigh high with stockings pure white, garter belts and all, topped off with the purest crisp white nurse's hat, carrying the sharpest most polished glittering pair of scissors, slowly moving toward his last vestige of humanity or "dog dum," however you want to see it . . . ahhhgggghhh! God noooo!

Well maybe I did dig a little deep into my favorite dreamed nightmare for all Black men who call my ladies "a bitch!" O yes, Black, do not start to think you are God because, as you know, "There's only room for one!"

When I say "Black" in this case I mean pointedly the "Black Woman" in all the facets where we find her. O yes, one point I need to touch on is the effort of trying to write "complexity" without committing the greatest of sins in the written word—that is to write it and that "without confusion!"

Let's hit this one spot and move on. That little tangent with the Black woman in the nurse's garb is exactly the problem we as Black men face oh too often. That was just plain "erotica" and I knew it while I was penning it. But once started, I fell into demon clothes as we are apt to do and I just went on and on. Well, I better stop or it will start again! Is this a universal thing or is it just another form of dog dum? No matter; I don't like to hear the B—word used in reference to y'all!

Time! Time! I call this here just to connect the dots. To show from whence I came and to see where I am trying to go.

I started with the statement, "I don't have two nickels to rub together, but I do have those three dimes somewhere in the mesh-mash of moving boxes, lost maybe forever. I don't really know." I just hope the luck they gave me year after year just lying there on my bureau gathering dust has not dwindled into oblivion with the lost sight of them!

It appears that in all my altruism, this novel really is all about us—this touted "Black America"—as if we were some foreign people that took root here with an embassy and all, oil wells, limo guards . . . you know the spill? Yet oddly enough, we've been here from the start, from the very beginning—the very impetus of American history!

The drum beats, the banjo, the rhythm, and the blues. From "Blues for Bessie" to the Blue Meridian, we have been right here. And just like the have-nots of the land . . . the "have-nots" you say? Well okay, the street people . . . the "street people" you say? Well all right, dog-gone-it, the dad-blasted derelicts—there, now I've gone and said it—the derelicts, the invisible souls of this great Christian society of ours. And do you know why I say "of ours?" It's because just like the Europeans that gave us Gospel loving Black folks our religion, we are just as guilty of walking by (or driving our Lexus by) one or all of these "invisible" and doing not one thing about their miserable condition; and have the nerve to shout and, yes, even pass out in the forefront of heaven while we practice the very concepts that says "love thy neighbor as you love yourself!"

I for one have not seen many derelicts driving a Lexus lately! Ah! But that is just one of my pet peeves.

You see, I can almost—and I say "almost"—understand why we as the greatest country in the world can as individuals and groups of individuals and as well as families sit and look at our plasma screen TV and chow down on steak, stall-raised beef, while watching some poor wretch, some Black woman who's flesh has turned to dry and withered skin stretched over her bones clutching a baby, the "hope of the world," hoping upon hope that someone will come and save the child from starvation and her from genocide in Darfur! After all, they're over there and we really don't know them and what can we do about it? Some even dare say, "They're Black!" There are some that even question, "Why do they keep having babies?" Well if they stop having babies, they're existence will be wiped out not in one generation but less than one decade! Make sense to ya? Huh? Does that make sense?

What kicks my anger into high gear is when I hear a news report that goes like this:

The Chinese now seem to be high rollers in the life and death struggle in Darfur! The Chinese in Darfur? What fur? Well it seems that all those dried human remains, the pointed photograph showing them lying in ditches and covered by dust and sand along almost any road there are lying on top of oceans of oil deposits beneath the ground. And guess what? The Chinese have, own, and buy 2/3 of all the oil produced there! Looks like some of that oil would at least buy the dead and dying of Darfur a decent hole in the blasted ground where they were born and have always lived! Ah, but no! In truth, it is even hinted that that great weaponry that the Army uses to kill unarmed farmers and goat herders is put in their hands by, you guessed it, "The Chinese!"

One thing that I've recognized over the years—or should I say the cognizant time of my 56 years—is that horrors over time take on themselves a kind of cinematic form of life within "self." "Make it clear, scribe!"

Well, if the likelihood of the ugliness continues and the unlikelihood of anyone doing anything about it lasts long enough, it starts to take on the image of martyrdom for a few. This martyrdom will, as it always does, start to rifle a few movie stars, tree huggers, animal activists, and the like to bring to the most advanced culture the knowledge that a few million people stand to die and have already died by the hundreds of thousands while we stood by and did not diddly-squat about it! "Invisible" millions just like the derelict that walks our streets every day. "Survive if you can," and if you can't . . . well, the meat wagon will collect your carcasses every morning. Unlike in "Darfur" Sudan where as "road kill" they are just left alongside the road to decompose and dry up, their skin sticking to their bones where the muscle had already ceased even before they were killed!

Why does this happen? Why does it continue to happen? A reason for you is that they have no real voice in the government of their land. In truth, most are like squatters on the land from whence they sprang! More importantly, they herd goats and sheep, grow miniscule crops on dry

53

and parched earth to feed the young that they keep having so they won't become "The Last Mohicans" of Africa!

This seems plausible but not feasible. The real reason being that they tend goats and crops and raise children, build that simple thatched roof house on top of oceans of "oil" that, by the way, the Chinese own 2/3 of all that is produced!

Why in the world are we fighting a war in Iraq that has flourished since before "Christ the King" and do not one godly thing about the "Darfur-ist?"

Oddly enough—and I hope you can begin to swallow this—it's for exactly the same reason. That part of Africa sits on oceans of oil. Anyone, any American, even our children, can tell you that practically all of the so-called Middle East is a mud puddle of pure "black crude!" It always surprised me—whether it be "Blood Stove" the movie or "Darfur Sudan" in real life or the OPEC supremacy of the Middle East—that it all must be mixed with proportionate parts of pure human blood to really make a pig's eye of difference to the world we live in!

I see admixture and I also see here in the Blue Ridge of the Virginias as it is all over the country that, for the need of correct posture, "the gouging at the gas pumps!" I must admit, I did not keep up with how many times the prices changed per gallon this year 2007, but I do know that for the better part, the price rarely fell anywhere close to the $2.00 mark. And just as an observation, every time about two months before any given holiday when the public will be traveling on the road going from hither to yon, the gas prices will jump well above $3.00 per gallon of gas; with most mid-size cars (that feed on this stuff which is refined from that crude with the blood admixture) having tanks that are at least 30-gallon capacity multiplied by the billions having an average 3.4 cars per household, we then can begin to realize the reason for endless war and needful genocide around this ole world of ours!

Why doesn't the Prez. do something about it? Well, Texas is not without oil itself!

It's tough to sit and watch on the Oprah Winfrey Show "Dwana Smallwood" defy gravity while sculpting and painting in no two same postures, flaunt perfection as the poetess pens the prose, the song! Her feet pointed like chisels threatening the floor as if to say, "I will to create just one more facet and you dare not move;" for my thighs bulk and shining, the muscles reflecting each wave of current lapping at the shores of my motherland, as my arms reach for Mount Kilimanjaro and my hands fling the wind something to embrace the fleeing birds of paradise rising in the setting sun of Africa! While the translucent cloth draping her torso fleeting wisp of fog allowing the dream to be viewed by the one asleep in perfumed beds.

All this? O yes, all this and this being only a moment in the presence of greatness, this crash definitive cry of joy!

Yet it does not stop. Here in the framework there appear out of the shadows into the light other young girls learning to dance—"Grace." Yes, and I guess that it can be said to even say "Grace" with the movement of each individual torso so lavishly blessed by "Alex Haley Dance School," Dancers Optimum!

I place this exquisite painting of voluptuous sable against the parched dead and dying flesh of Darfur and know that you, ("O" Black Woman: to dance happy in the face of our rival, poverty nor poverties cannot win; silver clouds roll like ships upon open sea horizons and our joy that perfect contrasting blue and earth smells that wonder of life of living "Black Woman" is you!)

<end excerpting>

The above paragraph is a line of verse from the poem "Nocturne" written 5/20/81 in the book of poetry penned *The Ebony Wood*; the title of which I've just set in print to be published. And by the time you read this novel (*The Days of the Three Dimes*), *The Ebony Wood* will have been published as well! Happy reading!! Larry Middlebrooks Sr.

I know the "Dimes" seems as though as some form of writing it should have ended with the above paragraph; but as the writer—or more the hands and eyes of this spirit that seems determined to be known—I know it has not nor cannot end here; and I really have no idea where or when it will.

I think it is time to begin again; for I am, as far as a novel is concerned, really in the truest form of the word without two nickels to rub together as for knowing what to write hither to for. Yet I know those same three dimes exist and somehow I know the luck they exude will pull me out of the moat and draw me nearer, "Near My Heart to Thee!"

Try this "word sandwich." I've tried without conscious knowledge to stay away from preaching. This being odd enough, for oddly I'm a preacher; and a preacher that does not preach is for the most part some kind of sin amongst all the other sins—a sin of sorts in itself!

It's hard to believe that on the circuit—that is, the preaching circuit—that there are entrance doors and exit doors that one may find himself standing at depending on his rise in the profession as it has become more of than a calling, which it should be than any other.

You see, when the young man or woman is "called" as we say it, he or she professes a moving by God Himself to share insights with their fellows that is not commonly known or seen by the rational man!

"Now, scribe, why would you use a combination punch like 'rational man?'"

Rational can only be seen as that thing accepted by the majority of those viewing any given subject as be subjective or real. You must forgive me at this point for here is where I wade in and the arms start to flail hoping to land a punch . . . a place where I can't even be called a novice fighter and stand totally in the shadow of the luck of the three dimes . . . a man merely seeking to survive a horrible fight, fighting never having fought before!

Rational man? In these times of war, peril, threats to blow up whole airports; small countries that have hate for the U.S. for breakfast! Such as North Korea and Iran playing with nuclear power while saying, "We don't have any other choice. We need this for energy and da-da-da; but if you don't be good to us, we may be able to create a B-O-M-B; but of course, we would never really dot-dee-dot-dot that because we're responsible!"

Now how did I get off on that? O yes, "Rational People!" Well it seems that in these times of such rational people, rational men are finding the import of God. And in His house are fewer and fewer of those called and a lot more of those trained in those hot houses for religious thinkers called "Bible College" than ever was before! And even though the schools turn out more and more professionals in the art of preaching, there seems to be fewer and less of the common literate man who finds the belief in God "rational!"

Which finds that one called by the traditional context standing right smack-a-dab in front of the exit door fighting for a chance to preach God and not television!

Now there you've gone and done it! You had to let the most covert word in the religious hierarchy out for the whole "public sector" to see! Why, if you're not careful, people may begin to see you as an infidel, some kind of infernal sinner!!

Somehow or another I find myself speaking to me during an in-depth self analysis of who and what I am as opposed to what I preach. Though I go flailing on totally unaware of what will happen when that well-planned, well-lain punch is landed by my opponent, the "secular Christian community!"

So here I stand before the door that has the glaring light of the word "exit" placed so very conspicuously above its aperture, daring me to take just one more step' knowing it will be all over for this old preacher. But being called and not trained, I still believe in the parting of the Red Sea and very little in "make up" and the right "camera angle."

I know, I know; it's all about reaching the most people. This would be well and good, but it seems that it has become the most people you can reach for the buck!

I think it's called on the street, "the most bang for the buck!" This proverb in itself is disquieting in that the words "bang for the buck" came from warmongers seeking the largest B-O-M-B they could find for the least amount of money; thus more "bang for the buck!" I never liked the word "buck." It seems that when it comes to "banging," it did not always apply to deer. Know what I mean?

God said, "Let there be light, and it was light."

"What are you trying to say, scribe? Are you asking a question or giving an answer?" For the reader of this word, be it novel or some kind of link, it may be a little of both! You see, these "Dimes" have again "broke" and the reins of this thriving beast have fallen from my hands and it is all that I can <u>do</u> to stay mounted as its mane flies in the wind. And with my head close to its neck, I can hear the flames and smoke ushering forth from its flared nostrils while the sparks break away at the stomping hooves on the way to places and ventures unknown! I want to just stop . . . nothing more; just stop and slide from this animal's back. But the more I scream, the faster it seems to move and it seems to joy in my loss of control!

As we run on faster and faster, the darkness starts to descend and a full silver moon seems to just sit on the near horizon. The trees fly by like ghosts and each specter is more ominous than the last until I feel as though I will lose consciousness . . . and do!

Such as it is with the "Dimes," from the couch to the pulpit, each place different; all things the same: I search each neuron and look around the contour of each. I find myself like you needing some old time religion. You know, the kind . . . well maybe you don't?

The modern generation is apt to think that the flashing lights and the camera close-ups, the spin out, the angle shot, the move in on that sweat droplet, the good . . . no, the excellent make-up job, the right suit or the sparkling dress to be "That Ole Time Religion," for it is the only religion they know!

"Religion?" Huh! That word is so ambiguous until it has become as scary as one of the old vampire movies of old. And just as likely to drain you of your blood . . . in fact, your blood supply, your wallet! What the heck? What have I got to lose? Even though I am a minister of the Gospel of Jesus Christ, I find myself standing before the exit sign and the door that says out!

You see, it doesn't pay to be too bold about "religion" these days! We have the righteous or those that hold to the idea that it is only proper to praise if you are conservative. Some even go as far as to say you only are right if you practice Catholicism and worship idol gods . . . oops, I mean spirits. And to the good Catholics, I mean no true or awful detriment! After all, I am just following the "Good Book." It does say, "Thou shalt take no gods before me!" Paraphrased! If we bow down to statues, are we not worshiping? Just a question.

Then we have those that propose that "We need the Spirit!" Some even make it clear and say the "Holy Spirit!" There seems although to be different types of Holy Spirit seekers. There are those that bounce off the walls "seeking the Holy Spirit" and there are those that "pass out!"

We have those that think we can bring a good song fest and bring the Holy Spirit along in the sound equipment. Don't get nervous, these are the ultra-ultra liberals! I find the search for God to be a venture within an adventure, one useful only if you have nothing really important to do—like the ones who look for the Spirit on Sunday and forget about it from Monday through Saturday. "Keep right on moving, scribe, to the left . . . to the left!" Next thing you know you'll be right out that exit door and God only knows what you'll find out there. After all, why do we need to stay in churches anyway? "What did you say? Scribe, scribe, don't you know the only reason we go church hopping is to find the Holy Spirit?"

"That's all right," wails the churches, whether conservative or ultra-ultra liberal. "We know your problem. You are an infidel and you've gone completely out of your infernal mind!"

I'll say to that, "I resent every word; but thank you very much because I can now go skipping merrily along, not having to be cautious and having to be accountable for nothing I say! Touché!

Yes, I suppose I could lean on the old insanity clause and at the same time escape punishment for my bold words against established and accepted religious beliefs. My problem—and I know that I have many—but at this point my real problem is that thing called and named "religion." And religion definition #2: the service and worship of God or the supernatural.

I also looked to definition "worship": reverence paid to a divine being; chiefly a person of importance; a title for various officials (magistrates and mayors).

Then I took the time to define supernatural: relating to God or demi-god, spirit, or infernal being; attributed to a ghost or spirit; eerie.

I think the last defining word tops the glass of imbuement off very nicely—for "religion" can truly be anything you deem it to be. Yet the Bible defines religion to the "eneteenth" (if there were such a <u>word</u>) level!

To fear the Lord and to do His own commandments; to serve Him and only Him; to come before Him with singing and gladness; to keep the Sabbath and make it holy; to love one another as with brotherly love; to observe the love of family and friend; to be sure to forgive one another of your faults; to chastise your children in love; to teach and be apt to teach at all times; to study the Word of God; and to live it with all perseverance: in this you will find true religion unfeigned!

The question is, "Are you there yet?" Yet in defining religion there was one ingredient praised that I didn't mention—the dollar—it looks like it has found its way into the chambers of worship as well! Well the idea was good but in actuation I find the trouble with Tribbles! As any good Trekkie will attest knowing—that when the Tribble came in contact with water, it was sure to multiply like "kettle corn put to heat," until it was not long until the Good Ship Enterprise was filled to the brim or rim with Tribbles! Thank God for Mr. Spock! I'm not sure, but I do believe that in one show they said something like, "It's up to God now!" I don't know, but it was something referring to a higher being, which brings us back to the original idea!

Sometimes we writers—and I take great liberty in saying "we"—yet the idea is to not let the striving beast get its own head and run away with you and the idea, too!

I'm still trying to prove . . . I'm still trying to write my heart. And at this juncture my heart is against electronic preachers wearing their make-up and eye shadow because now it has become all about "Do I look good? Is there any shine on my nose? Are the shoes I'm wearing okay?" This kind of rattle trap bull makes me sick! Does God look good? After all, it's His show . . . or was!

Now I no less than others believe in reaching the multitudes; and that is exactly why Jesus sent forth His disciples two by two—one to support the other in weakness, but more to preach and gain to the heart and arms of God; to snatch from ole Slew Foot, the "Devil," the multitudes.

We were originally supposed to follow Jesus' example in all things, including his death! Oh! You thought it was easy, huh? Cadillacs, Rolls Royces, silk shirts, Italian suits, $5,000,000 homes, two wives, and assorted staff! O forgive me, I meant one wife and assorted staff, with some staff doing assorted jobs!

Preacher, we have become Sadducees and Pharisees and not a whole lot more! You see, we know the Letter of the Law we teach and we can be seen practicing it on TV, radio, and even movies and computers (desk tops and lap tops); but I'm afraid that while we were studying the Word, a spam popped up and said something like "Nude, Black chick with a white guy doing the foulest and most blissful exotic things that your little fat-eyed seething mind can imagine . . . click here."

The Internet: "Hell has truly enlarged her mouth to swallow our waste by products of sin!"

Some preacher is sitting at this very moment trying to figure out how to form his lips into the words that say, "I didn't do it. I didn't know what it was. I just glanced at it once!"

Damn, why can't we admit that we have been snared by the Devil? Or are you at the gates of Sainthood already? Wake up! You're not about to fool Jesus. Not this time!

We as preachers better wake up and realize it's time for Judgment; not making multi-billion dollar extravaganzas!

When it's time for a "conference," the flashing lights, the loud music, that announcer with the perfect voice, the pan in, pan out shots of the up and coming entertainment rival Broadway Hacktees panning "Live sex on stage for all to see . . . step right up, come right in. Get your doves right here. No, over here—I'm selling spotless sheep. No, over here—I have special anointing oil. Over here . . . over here . . . over here . . . no, turn to our channel—we have the truth!"

What is the truth? The truth is that I have "clicked" right there and I looked! I shook my head, I shivered, and I looked. After some time, the shivers stopped! Before I knew what was going on, my head stopped shaking, my eyes stopped rolling with distaste, and I found myself just looking. And in all honesty, I found myself hoping a pop-up would appear and I was glad when it did. But what's worse is when the pop-up didn't appear, as they say, "By God, I went searching!"

The truth is "It's time for the examination. It's time for the Judgment." Judgment, my brothers, begins at the House of God! Are you ready?

The truth is we need Jesus to come with his plaited cords and whip the fair pee out of us until we wake up and remember why He called us in the first place!

Get up from that hypnotized lull that this society that Satan has created with its just so close borders of sin, dancing every so lightly like a moth around a candle flame! Have you ever been so lucky as to watch a moth lose control, stop flapping its tuxedo, and go spiraling dizzily into the flames? You ever laugh at the puff of smoke that was life only seconds before?

Jesus is on the way back; and like that moth, we at end in the House of God will stand before Jesus the Righteous Judge and our sins, the same sins that we think "That's not so bad," will judge us.

Preachers, we haven't lost it. We are not so sinful that we can't be saved, and we are not so sinful until we can't lead the way to the redemption cross and to the One who gives salvation freely! For indeed if "salvation" is free, Jesus bought it for us when He died on the cross at Golgotha; but what's even more important is He insured it when He arose from the grave! Not if . . . not maybe . . . not the "factor" . . . but the divine truth! I didn't meet Jesus in the Bible. I was blessed to meet Him on the road from "flapping my wank!"

Sin is hard; life is hard; but life is hard because of sin! Getting around sin is impossible! Overcoming sin is a learning process that by looking again and again at the examples Jesus left we can possibly overcome them one at a time and thereby grow stronger each time!

Yet it is very important to understand that you will, by the "craftiness of the flesh," back slide!

Don't stop fighting the good fight for with endurance we will . . . yes, "we" will gain our crown!

Remember, when and with your preachment, "the race is not given to the swift nor the battle to the strong; but to him that endures until the end!" You know, I just wish that I could speak to some of those that went on before. I wouldn't ask them about golden streets nor slippers or mansions. If that's all heaven was about, I may as well stay on earth or even "go to hell!" No, I would ask them what kind of sins did you commit and how did you deal with self once it had conceived? Because I know that when sin has conceived, it bringeth forth death; yet you did not die immediately, but you have died; although death is the outcome and the outcry of all men! How did you stand yourself afterward? This question seems all of import, because people, unless they have a reprobate mind, usually suffer horribly with the accusation of the sin act, no matter how big or small!

I say big or small, yet I know there is no "big sin" or "little sin." For sin is sin! You can go to hell for stealing a fountain pen as easily as committing adultery. And committing adultery is as easy as casting a lustful eye at the woman in the front pew who always wears the reddest and the shortest, most low-cut cleavage dress that, that Devil of a dress maker could make!

Sin is, after all, sin!

At this juncture, I want to say: you guys, yes, you preacher, it may feel strange but you are not alone in this architecture of lies, deception, and public and private expectation that has a tendency to roll into a small whimpering ball and carry us along like Pecos Bill riding the proverbial "whirlwind" cactus and all!

The import here is not that we do wrong; it's what we have the nerve to do about it! You ever notice how a practicing preacher that has done wrong and God convicts him or he gets caught in the act, how when he steps out and publicly announces his or her wrong, the weight that seems to lift off everyone after the expected great "sur-pise" passes and how quickly they are forgiven?

It appears that we need to know that our ministers every now and then are human, too! This does not give credence nor the authority to sin;

but it does remind us that our Lord said, "I will never leave you nor forsake you; even to the end of the world!"

With this kind of assurance, I can find the nerve to say it and say it all, let alone "write my heart!" So fight on, Christian soldier, fight on! We'll win yet. Matter of fact, I read the end of the book and we already have! All else is merely an illusion. That's all, just an illusion!

Then you say if it all is an illusion, then why does it hurt so very much? "It?" Yes, "it"—this reality we call life! "It" hurts. This almost sounds like the cry I've heard uttering on some TV show about fatherly sexual abuse of his tiny daughter. "It hurts," the child cries in torment to an unhearing, uncaring, vicious rapist, the spittle and foam around his drunken booze breathing mouth! "It hurts," cried out to the only protector she's ever known, the same father that has bounced her on his knee time and time again, the same father that would touch her flat chest and tell her how much she has grown and rub her in the place when she was under the cover with the whisper, "Don't tell Mamie; it's just our little secret, okay?" "Okay, Daddy," giggling in that childish manner in just the way that sets these kind of monsters on fire with unabated ravishing animal lust. Lust thought about, felt, and nurtured until in the night he sneaks into the little one's bedroom and she cries, "it hurts," with his hand over her mouth! Now time and time again until she cries no more!

This is graphic, yes! But how many little girls suffer the atrocity with no one to defend their little bodies let alone their rights as female children and most of all humans? We may ask the question, "Who was the first one to call you bitch?" Do you remember or has time washed it from memory?

I was watching the Oprah show today like I take time to do on most days. Only on this day she had many of the hip-hop artists and a smattering of the greatest moguls that exist in modern time representing the hip-hop industry as a whole. The questions and answers were varied; but the centerpiece as I settled was how the art—and I don't use the word "art" loosely because it is just that—an art! An art that is as significant as spray painted walls that just said we are hurting here and we are hurting there; the same art that the police would chase us away from defiling someone's property in the ghetto (probably our own) if for no other reason than we have squatter's rights; for we have lived, died, born, and buried there generation after generation—"it must belong to us for I don't see anyone else living there, live out there but us!"

Now as time and tide have told, this simple graffiti has become the nomenclature for the city streets and has ascended to the very heights of art itself to the point great photographers stop by and take photos of the art and the artist at work, for we can no longer call it play! It is history in the culmination, the conception, and the birth. And if you listen closely, you can hear the babe crying ever so lively from the "crib," of this I am certain, hip-hop is here to stay no matter the form it comes in. It is a valid reality!

Question: "Why do they use so many 'bitches' and 'hoes' in that kind of sound?" Is it a possibility that this is retro-productive and counter accomplishment? Well maybe. But in order to be sure, we have to go back to the heart and mind of *The Days of the Three Dimes*. You see, the "Dimes" started out whipping butt! What kind of butt, you may ask? Well I'm glad you asked! You see, the "Dimes" were bold enough to question: "Did you wipe your butt? If you didn't, well why not?" This, of course, is a metaphoric question and it is here because of the quest!

We could care less! Yes, we can care less and indeed this in itself is the very root of the problem.

We can be seen as a people locked away in poverty and degradation caring less! Or a people not bright enough to know we need to care more! Or a people who are so tired of opinions they act like concrete boots in a lake and drag us under kicking and screaming with people listening until our hands are under water at which time they walk away, with the accepted relief that it is too late; and like a burlap sack of unwanted kittens, we push the image down into our subconscious and forget the whole dirty mess!

Unfortunately the ghost of all the Black men and women who were forced down in this society are called upon by the great seers of this, our society. You see, every time a Black graduates and gets that diploma or that degree, the ghost rises in resounding applause and it will not let us forget!

We are human feeling beings, yes, and we will rise!

"Then, scribe, what seems to be the problem?" Well it's our music. It seems that like the "Black bottom" of long ago "twenties" and the years of "hop," it just too vulgar. It's just too suggestive! Suggestive of what? <u>Sex</u>. Yes, sex! Now you've gone and done it again! You used the word! Shhhh! Someone might hear you. You know, the kids and the next door neighbors. It doesn't matter. In today's time we have sex education in primary school!

It doesn't matter that because we didn't have sex education, HIV and Aids run rampant in the Black race and the Black culture around the world. And, if we are ever going to overcome—and I do mean overcome in every area of endeavor—we are going to have to be taught:

Sex and all things that pertain to human life (not just the existence) but the living of life!

You see, the Black realized long ago that the incorporation of sex into their style of life is just being real! After all, from it springs life. Now wait a minute. You see, from it springs life but for the poor Black and writhing upward ascending Black, it is the very stuff of his enterprise itself! Yes, I know. "It's tight, but it's right!"

You see, that bedroom was just the beginning of the insult to the Black female. Her bodily abuse has gone on since she was a servant and a slave in the Black queen's and the Black king's court. In many cases that goes as far back as Solomon himself!

The lesser cast group even in the Black ruling world was given the task of pleasing the queen, who just happened to be Black, or the king, who just happened to be Black, and the ruling party; and this was part of their right as royalty!

Wait a minute. Wait a minute. You mean to tell me there were Black kings and queens? An emphatic yes!

Well how could they treat their own people like that? The answer is found in the history of all modern day kings and queens in the culture of the Caucasian races. The lower cast groups were burdened with such tasks and still are. And it is an accepted norm! When I say modern day monarchy, I mean the 8th Century until now in the 21st Century. Things haven't really changed that much now have they?

There is one thing that has changed and that is the predominance of kings and queens in the Black race. Although they still exist but with eminence as of time preceding modern kingship and queens reign today.

"Scribe, get on with it." Well I've taken time to lay some concrete groundwork for our reasoning when it comes to our position on <u>sex</u>! It seems that Black women have always been the object of men's most delightful and many times his most distasteful desires. Why heck, the woman's got it! Whatever it is, the Black woman has just got IT! Being Black, I could be somewhat prejudice; but in all history, she has come first . . . always!

The problem arises in this: That in the overlapping cast groups, the queens have been lost amongst the bed warmers (who, by the way, had no little degree of respect until she came to America as a slave)! Our women were not dissed until they came here to these shores.

I used to wonder what kind of woman would fling herself over the side of a ship in the awaiting arms of the sea to be drowned. The answer at last: Queens!

They would rather die than to be treated like mere chattel by any man! They never knew of it and they would never learn!

What's that got to do with hip-hop and the hip-hop culture? Well, nothing and everything! You see, Black women were beaten, raped, molested, belittled, twisted, and torn long before they became proper money-making prostitutes (who, by the way, in the early years were needed by many families as bread winners and were quietly respected for feeding the little ones by grandma and grandpa who couldn't get a job)!

Well they may get a job cleaning behind Uncle Charlie and cleaning spittoons! By some form of natural ascension by dissensions way, these were the same men that the white men turned to when they wanted some chocolate delight every night!

"You see, once you go Black . . . ," well you know the saying. To move on, this process of special pleasures has not expired; but indeed, like the painted graffiti, the art of pleasure has transpired and has become an inspiration for millions of men, women, young boys and girls, across the cultures and races! What was once graffiti has become the most ludicrous art. Now about these bitches and hoes . . . it's really hard to say who called her a bitch first. We may never know whether it was uncle or his son, Big Tim the slave, or Mother Lois who expected her to go out and sell her body to provide for the family because, as far as beauty or brains she may have—and I say may have—lacked in both arenas; or maybe it was the father who crept into your bedroom on some dark, evil shadow cast night while you cried, "Daddy, it hurts!"

Maybe it was the United States of America and the pressures it puts on Blacks, men and women, to survive any way, any how, at all cost, and at all times to survive!

The thing about this race called "Black" is that they have an uncanny ability to improvise and survive. By God they will, yes, survive! Survive because we must!

The beast has slowed it's traverse and I can feel my heart pounding, resounding across the dunes as *The Days of Three Dimes* begins to play its tunes.

At first it is the gentle whistle of an ocean breeze blowing through the conch . . . then Conbrio!

Watching sweating Blacks, polka dot kerchiefs, lively colors picking cotton, laughing tunes, the babies cry, bare feet, and straw hats wetting the dew.

The striving, strided beats that beast gallops long into the sun rising mosaic gold, nothing pretty yet just thoughts of the motherland told by a taupe motif and arranged in Latry, The Laureate Rhyme!

Sing celebrant if you dare, we that seek the Christ do care. Sing, o sing the laity doth make us the happy, merry people ole: Daub and chink be filled our hearts overflow and now this:

6. "Remember, O Lord, thy tender mercies and thy loving kindness, for they have been ever of old.
7. "Remember not the sins of my youth nor my transgressions according to thy mercy, remember thou me for thy goodness sake, O Lord.
8. "Good and upright is the Lord; therefore will he teach sinners in the way.
9. "The meek will he guide in judgment; and the meek will he teach his way;
10. "All the paths of thee are mercy and truth unto such as keep his covenant and his testimonies.
11. "For thy name's sake, O Lord, pardon mine iniquity, for it is great.
12. "What man is he that feareth the Lord? Him shall he teach in the way that he shall choose.

Loose these chains, society doth wrest, while Christ doth plait a three-fold cord and whip these selling the knowledge of "tiresias" the soothsayer old! And pigeons are sold to praise piety.

<end excerpting>

67

We, the Black race, have tasted the musty odor of this saprophytic life. We survive on this dying spice:

Leaping from sailing ships and standing naked upon the blocks of urbanism, living the tenant in halls, maturate, drunken, divisive crack heads urinate!

If only Uriel real shun the blath; make sense of rising sunsets we pray, "scribe," into the falling sunrise that sits at high noon as this rock is warmed by the blaze:

Orange orb blaspheme if we dare ask why our woman must suck at the altar lain of golden silk and sheets of satin we milk, her the diadem ware; the chalice care her thighs consummate, to only contact her soul! We conspire to wrap her hair in the conical knot from pigtails she wear, as we swear upon this the holy writ.

Old men sitting watching her new robust blooming, like a peonies each bloom, sweet nectar we strain to see her bend to take water from the well. No sin we seek her and other men so!

This striving, striding Black beast, nostrils flared and his flanks knot against my thighs as we ride!

A flowing tide washing up upon the sand a body of a Black man long since drowned in social remorse! Its symphony calling out loudly with the tilted drums in between his legs, an open mouthed scream—yelling about social chains and ethnic lapse of minority beliefs. So she lavages her only trading stamp and seeks for tomorrow while fending her "captured HIV!"

The leading edge of fallen ebony, Nubian pride. Her breast set high upon the mount of "Ingidy" as the word pseudonymous her plight reality score!

Now regress backward stance; find her regal, I implore! Don't leave us on this road to Paradise to find a fresh photo of porno refutation: for I know there is more!

After all, this score of dismantled blame is not to be seen but the only way it can "Lilliputian Pursuant" to our fall, when in reality our women, our men, our boys and girls stand gigantic all; not some "tall!" After all, the pain this laudanum to ease its searing rage.

Rage: why not, for it is many things, this book of Dimes. Let it whisper. Let it cry and reticulate its lines of joy and pain. Let it employ the Black man's brain; sometimes this, "the one act play," lasting for all eternity!

[Rage] comes upon <u>me</u> quite without warning while I sit in the quiet "wood." It comes over me dark and flows over me hot like molten lava.

That God give beneficence has flown, and those dark and loathsome whispers that I am wont to hear stay with me.

Whispering of insane things, insane places, and insane deeds.

I fight against their "absorbing the me into them 'until' I am no more!"

Crowding in betwixt my ears taking lavatory in my grey matter; indelibly printing on my brain, whispers, "psychic, psychic, psychic, insane!"

Until she makes me erect with talk of her most private being, leading me by my libido through corridors lain in libertine.

My prayers are unanswered as they cling to my soul. The voices like vines smother me, trying to destroy my being.

She laughs often times with maniacal malignant glee affecting all that hear her with a sickness of the lost soul, and I play the fool, for my lust for the "promised oasis" called satisfaction, [her body] is as great as the lust for the knowledge of who she is and who they are that mind collectic (PSI).

It is she; for the voice is female inside my head. She deceives me, leading me a little, so as to know my strength, my weakness, and my dread.

To think that we use to laugh and talk without me ever seeing her, (PSI) hidden out of physical sight.

Now I racked in pain, my body taut, tense in shame while fearing self destruction. I try to take my own life four times in four years. I only know my name!

Often I revert to self-abnegation leaving my hair uncombed and my body unclean.

In this way she bethinks to hold me, my mind at her will's command, my body inside convulsing from fear and distaste of my inner being.

I find myself hating myself for ever allowing myself to be fooled into believing that (PSI) is "just," torn alone I die while (PSI) looks on.

(I often weep inside, dry teardrops.) "God is hiding." I promised to stop myself abuse, but I cannot while she has me. She caresses sooo gently. She tells me to die and I do!

PSI teases while telling her guiltless lies, all the defending; her ploy built on the context that her pain given is joy!

The screaming never stops. Sometimes I scream aloud until without conscious knowledge my voice level drops and I find my screaming inside!

I am in you and you are in me. We are one; all that exists and in us there is all.

Her lie is sweet. She bethinks to enslave my very <u>soul</u>. She wants to use me as a "guinea pig" so that she might find ways to enslave others with her brain!

"Her planned deceit in continuity:" give in, don't fight, come fly with me to eternal heights. [[(I love you, Larry!)]], she says.

Moderate

So I curse her existence, for I do not know her name; I damn her soul and I accuse her until my eyeballs red and veined, pop, and I go insane, listening never seeing!

I try to tell others about her abuse—"mental it is true"—but what is a man except his mind? What is the hourglass without the sands of time?

But they won't believe me and they all ask the same damn, dumb questions—who is she, where is she, what's her name?

I don't know her name! How could I know her name? All I do is hear and speak to her and beg her to leave me alone. No! Demand that she leave me alone!

I attend the counsel of the doctor, the scientist proper, and the theologian too. None of them can find anything wrong. They don't know what to do.

I have never seen her. All I know is that she makes slaves of man's mind; then she drives them insane with ambiguous sexual babble.

I spend my days at home in a semi-dark delirium; alone I weep, for God I search!

When I knock, He is not at home so the door cannot be opened.

When I ask where He is, no one knows and there is no need of asking.

When I seek, I find myself going in circles chasing my own fears!

I scream "Lilith" into the pitch darkness—goddess of night, goddess of sex, and for wont of a better name, I call (PSI) goddess of debauchery!

I pray to God. I gather strength but when I am alone and done praying, she acts as the unwanted succubus draining me:

<end excerpting>

Smile, O daughter of mine. Your black satin skin is never forgat. I know of your spaceless flight over sand dune and jungle loam, the height of a world you carry in your bosom blessed O times numeration conscious thine revenant "bless your return" O luscious your basket fruit: velvet breast; this [nocturne] to every Black woman that every lived!

"Black woman denude" in this thy graces for to light these shadows do veil your sacred heart;

Between nocturant romance, thine on sinewy muscle do bind my spirit with labors through the slave hardship won our life; for food the love you nurture in your heart and each tear falling cleansing my wounds, malign throans do not bend my will; unto you all my saving lost dreams renew "you" upon each kiss:

Black woman to weave thine tapestry from reed grass and wipe my fevered brow, upon the mat and lap do kindle my heart's, body, and soul's desire.

To suckle at velvet breast a babe—delusions wash from these mire—infant bone and alone you walk in aging wonder black eyes to see!

Thwart these chainless wrists do wait and wane my anger. Rhapsodies of love, the nightingale's song in late evening rushes and hollow places and Georgia swamps those (shades) ghost paling skin do glow through sightless eyes for your lasting trust Black woman! To score your skin of black and velvet to underscore your name!

I write, "I love you, your son, lover, friend, enemy, and man;" and through my rushing blood do flow with mighty burst from heart The River Sphinx, "Niger," does sing the hard and setting sun's "reflecting hues from its dark like night glassy surface and night birds wing on silent paths joyous moon beams and starlight dust, dine with hue in dusty shadows, your dusty feet have walked long." Your rain fall's songs of heart and harp!

Melodic vibes teasing me into felted peace, "O Black Woman," making my bed, my bread, feeding us from bones they have passed away as no good, to nourish us to full prayerful meal.

When all was lost, to stand upon each street to speak of your heartfelt sorrows alone! If we live through cosmic rays reaching always outward to thine own heart, the star and crown, O Black Woman, O Magi, work ye that lasting magic and cool my heated words; for in anger I sometimes forget that you earth, sun, and rain sing silver notes from each strand of being!

How you have watched on aching days your "men" walking with another of lighter hue.

If only we knew your waiting hope no longer to linger in euphoric opiant dream illusion.

The song wave upon wave, to oboe upward into flute, dancing away on tilted Congo drums beating away disenchantment, leaving behind the enchanted heart on that sparkling platinum ray of light.

O Black fold after fold on Black velveteen backdrops the early morning sky, in dew the East moistened, in the afternoon withered grass of brown, lone ebony trees stand, open prairies, families of ancient times!

Also together they sing the oneness of heart and soul, spirit and mind, to breathe want together is to known the happiness of satiated need!

To dance happy in the face of our rival—poverty cannot win. Silver clouds roll like ships upon open sea horizons and our joy, that perfect contrasting blue and earth smells, that wonder of life of living, O Black Woman, is you!

<end excerpting>

Ahhhh! These velvet, these Black women, and so much more: "The Dimes" just lying there upon the dusty old chest, keeping time and good luck . . . no, not luck, but history! For you see, the original "dimes" have gone into another place and the "three dimes" I see now laying just so, divided in equal distance on the window sill, are new dimes, not old; and I guess their quality has carried over to these new days as well.

I thought for a long time that by letting the first three lay there that they would bring me luck, "since my so-called luck has been so bad lately," saith the scribe! Yet I've noticed no real change in my position or my condition. I've really lost nothing and I feel more like "S.J. Got Rocks" on this day than any other, the 28th day of June, 2007. Yes, S.J. is my name . . . old, "Seeking Jesus" got rocks!

Why Got Rocks? Well like most of us in this beautiful race, we're still seeking Jesus and we don't know how to find . . . thus the reason for Got Rocks: instead of Plentitude, we just Got Rocks!

I'm a minister, which doesn't say much because in essence we are all ministers if we care for the needs of our brother and sister. O, I don't mean the same vain work nor the same blood line, not even the same race, but the same creator of us all. And that's hard to say because that includes every race of men . . . yes, even the Caucasian! The bold Caucasian! Quick to say "Nigger" and even quicker to ask a Nigger doctor to save his life!

"Now, scribe, even though you don't want to admit, you've stepped over into another vane, another moveable venue, in that the question is posed, 'So you think you can dance?'" My answer comes quickly as I waltz around the hairy issues of race opposing race rears its ugly head. It always did and it probably always will even though we may ascend to a level of "justice prevails" where the question is answered in just good will games . . . I believe the rivalry will always be there in that. I don't believe we will ever become just a cup of creamed coffee—"if you know what I mean"—no matter how sweet it is. This touching and intermingling of the super races—white/Black or Black/white! Uhmm! Is this "numerologically calculable?"

No matter what pie graph you use, it always comes to whom is best—you Poe or is that Pooo; you just Po—and it really doesn't matter what your skin may be. Now if you rich like capital "O" Rich, your color becomes "synonymous and systematic theology!" In that the art of maintaining the racial purities is lifted so high it seems to vie with the many socialized religions of the world. It stands forth—yes, "erect"—and prominent in its quest for who is greatest or biggest or largest or longest running in the world; and maybe who may be smallest (referring to the pigmy, of course). Uhmm! Is this synonymous also? No pun intended.

Maybe this is the reason that the female of all races seems to get along so much better than their male counter parts; in that the vibrating energy is used at times by all! Which gives rise to the likelihood that all women are truly "intuit" of the innate nature that is "woman."

"Let me see," said the blind man to his brother! This statement is probably the culmination of all the thoughts that bring about propagation of the ideals of the futility on teaching races to move from prejudicial concepts, the infinite rationale that continues in spite of all the lessons; man seems to cling to all of his expiatory beliefs for purity amongst the races . . . or is this just—excuse me—like to raise hell?

There are not a few hellish people practicing "old school" policies in the name of purity! That's why I cited the "intuit" innate nature of women—it seems they could care less about in actuality "power holds," and they would much rather just get along!

Matter of fact, their greatest argument arises when another woman wears the same dress! It seems they have not arisen to the height of bigger bombs! Uhmm! I wonder, could this be because of their phallic phantasm or maybe it's that they don't gauge their "fruit tree"—at all!

After all is said and done, living in the southern part of the nation has allowed me to see some major changes that those of old never thought would ever be!

It may have begun with the "Daniels Band" or go as far back as "Snoop & Scoop" introducing the up and coming Roy Rogers western show for the five o'clock TV show, or even the greatest crossover artist ever born in the form of the illustrious "Kid Rock!" "Why, scribe, why? Who do you cite these space and time travelers?"

These ratavis beings have as those well before been the harbingers of the greatest metamorphosis of social change:

Music, no matter where it hails, always denotes its society and the social construct and its changing nature. If this being so, then the South is experiencing the utmost in growing pangs of any natural act in humanity!

Therefore it is no surprise that we get along and treat each other with some degree of dignity while plotting with dignity a lynching or a razoring of someone's throat if caught in the wrong alley way!

"Scribe, now scribe, why did you go and say that?" Because it's true and to journal change is to tell the truth even though it may not be timely or comfortable. I never thought a razor felt good and I'm sure a rope even less!

Here's what brings me to this conclusion. Everyone knows or at the very least feels some kind of under surface rumbling; and every now and then some poor soul pays the price for it! It's not openly known as it was in the old days, but it goes on just the same!

Sometimes people are lost during high days of celebration such as days of carnival and parade, never seen again and no one asks where these little children are!

"Scribe, if children are lost, it would seem that someone would miss them and know." This is a true word, but children that are lost are not always children in the true sense of the word. And the only reason that I cited this difficult situation is that it signifies things that go on in this country right in our presence and most of us don't even know it is happening!

Take for example—and this is not to "beat a dead horse to death" but to emphasize a reality why America has changed—the world has changed, changed dramatically all around us. Either we are born into a new climate and it is normal and natural, or we have become numb by the process, or we are too old and too deaf and dumb to hear a reality that exists like the satellites in space. I refer to the way we communicate. We talk mind to mind now better than we do on our Chocolate or our Blackberry. And I assume that it is supposed to be some kind of secret. No, I know that it is some kind of secret! But like puss oozing out of an infected wound, this society is effected and affected by its upward and outward mobility. And just like that, sure it stinketh and its growing pangs hurt, and that off-scouring of "where are the races supposed to stand" now is just as un-ignorable as the puss oozing from a putrid sore!

Personally, just like the Black woman, who is by my standards ideal when it comes to leadership, and her white counterpart, whom we all know is set and fixed in the arena of brains and that economic brawn, it's almost as scary as the late night horror movies to think as a world we may have to give to a matriarch society just to survive our own self-made destruction.

The only thing I dread with this possible scenario is their choosing of the connubial mates for that import of <u>offspring</u>. You see, I am not "all that!" But I have my assets if I am really moved toward exhibiting them, if you know what I mean. I mean I can be (as I am sure many of us are), "We can be activated by the right stuff!" "The right stuff?" Humm! Have I digressed to the place I deem to escape from? That being plain old male, sweet male chauvinism! "Now stop right there, scribe. That was a cheap shot at the male race." No, not really. And I say not really because I am the last one on the face of this earth to put myself in the position to be called a cheap-jack. After all, these are not cheap articles I deal with here. For I know and you know, "women and men," that women of today don't come cheap. Matter of fact, if you think they will, you just may run across one or two that will just set you in your place and tell you, "I just won't come at all!" What you do then? What else? Tuck your tail, bow your head, and say, "Just wait till I get back!" Of course that's what you'll say. Today's woman ain't cheap; neither was yesterday's. Being women, they just didn't throw their weight around. By the way, have you noticed how they always seem to win?

Now it may seem that I am some kind of "Judas" to my many male "likes;" but the oddity is that when a male starts talking like this, people either think that he is a masochist wanting and needing a spanking by his female counterparts; he's a homosexual; or he's thrown in the towel, gone out of his mind, and given over completely to the female genre—"A mamma's boy" or just a Spanky!

In reality, women outnumber by some hectic percentage that keeps changing—and today, July 3, I don't even know what it is myself. But I do know from birthing mothers to astronauts, women are not to be taken lightly . . . . "The hand that rocks the cradle." It's true. She may bake pies but she also rules the world!

Here's a reality: men who speak on women this way, you would think is some kind of social persona or literate on the sexes and that the female gender would just eat it up. Don't be fooled, my friend (that is, if I'm still your friend). Women are very cautious and, when they find a man that knows that today, they prefer the sexual stimulation of "stilettos" today and the suave and de-boner of that sexy "wedge" the next sometimes—for that man throw him into the pit of retro trust and have him under the protective eye of the "Amazonian" leaders of the gender and find himself in the sticky lips of the greatest Venus fly trap in the world and under no little scrutiny by them all; and by the word "all" I mean "all"—every female of every race, creed, and national origin!

No, it is not a given. It is indeed a tedious and fragile walk to even think you know as a male "females!" In fact, you may find yourself living a very stercoriclous life style—you know, living in and at the very least being dung!

Let's change a gear or two as we speed down this road of social economics. Let us not find ourselves "pound-foolish." That is, let us not find ourselves imprudent in dealing with large matters so as to think that the answers are even attainable at all. For you see, I as this scribe am not trying to resolve some sexist point of view. Quite the contrary. I'm just giving the just dues where they may fall!

It seems that whenever anything as change came to be, in truth we can find its roots in Femme Fatel!

I found myself in the sanctuary today giving the Omnipotent One His just dues, in that He just by chance created all things. And if the spirit of these "Dimes" are ever to be controlled, it won't be by the hand that meets the sensorum face to face or wields this pen that will have the honor of saying, "I controlled it!"

This striving beast gallops on and tramples down those <u>grapes</u> of wrath we hear about. No, the flanks of this beast are far too strong and his head has been in the wind for far too long now to draw him into a stop. No, we must ride on, the wind whispering by our ears, even sometimes it screams as it passes to the place we were!

I found myself looking around the sanctuary and as usual I found it so odd to see so many well-dressed, some beautiful, some okay, and some not but females look toward the altar and the pulpit waiting for the guiding Word of God it was women!

In truth, the will of the church is truly embodied in women. It is no surprise that the "fall of man" began with a woman, and the gateway for man's saving grace came by and through a "woman's womb."

It's seemingly odd that when we view the church, we see so many men at the helm! Church leadership is by all appearance in the hands of men, but—and I say but—if we really do live in a democratic society and the majority doth rule, then whom are we really fooling? Every church in America and around the world is filled with female bodies! We men are the small minority! Uhhh! Step up, bend over, and remember the first spanking came from Mom who popped our little hands when we refused to pay attention, and it will be a woman too who will give us the ultimate whipping to get all of us in line with the true will of God if we are ever to be saved! It will take the female to navigate us through troublous straits; it will be the female who we will call the troubadour that writes the music for our accomplished task that she led us through!

As a man, it is true that I am just as affected by the petticoats as the next man; but as a man seeking the higher power, I am very afraid and this is most of the time!

You see, I don't like to see or hear men, my brothers, downgrading the female. I really find my ears aching when I hear men say some of the things men say and think. It's like someone running fingernails across a chalkboard!

By the way, this is the reason I'm so very afraid! When I look out over the church, I can't allow my "man" to rise up and exhibit itself. I can't be a man in church as men are, as men can be when we are affected by the female genre. "Be very careful, scribe, you are heading toward quicksand and indeed you already have one foot immersed." Today, yes, this day, I saw women that clearly outnumbered the men and it was what had been enunciated as "Men's Day!"

I saw clearly through these mortal eyes and I am ashamed that the eyes I saw through were not completely spiritual; but I saw women dressed in the most lovely fashion and they "needed" a "good man!"

Yet the Bible declares there is none "good" but God! Then are they looking for God or good in some "please Lord," find me a "good man!"

Now don't get me wrong . . . women don't just go to church looking for a man. But I have heard the summary that if you need a good man, go to church! Go to church? Come on; how can you go to church to find a good man when even I looking out over the church am afraid to really look? Yes, I am ashamed and I am wrong. Yes, I am a man. Have I sinned? I do think so.

You see, the reason I injected this odd input here is because we all—men and women—have this weakness. When we take off our church clothes, no matter how good a Christian we think we are, we at earth level need the opposite sex. And if we are not very careful, it will get in the way of our praise! Oh, I know your fists are up and you are ready to fight. But God not man created "man" . . . "he them" and "she them." We are naturally drawn to one another. Yet I have seen excessive activity disguised as Christian social serve gatherings. It's no wonder so many preachers are overcome by women who have the greatest need in the hotbeds of thought of a good tumble in the sheets!

Is it any wonder we teach and preach and tremble?

What I am trying to say without putting my foot in my mouth and taking and making the positive outlooks to become some sort of lie is simply "we need one another," and not just as Christian partners, but lovers and friends!

Yet in essence, in order for our root stock and means to work, we need our anchor to hold in the veil. In other words, if it's going to be right, it needs to begin and stay with God!

I look out over the world congregation and the Black Epoch unfolds as I watch the ultimate leaders, movers, and shakers in our society and I see beautiful Black women that just decided that "this is the way it needs to be done!"

Not all of these women have always been married to some strong Black man figure. No, in truth, they were the strong "Black figure," and I don't think that anyone in America has not been truly moved and affected and effected by one of these queens and at the very least an empress through their walk in our society as well as the world society! "Now, scribe, that's saying an awful lot seeing that none of those women have ever been crowned!" Well maybe not in the regal fashion, but in the fashion of queens they truly are. Just to name a few:

Dr. Prophet Juanita Bynum. Here is a woman that stood up out of the dust bowl of life at the moving of God on her spirit, mind, body, and soul and wrapped in sheets could bring congregations to their feet in tears of joy and praise!

She preaches, teaches, sings, prophesies, and leads Black women from the alley to the altar! Why? Because Dr. Bynum has been in all places at one time or another. She knows the effect and the affect drugs and alcohol can have in the degeneracy of the Black woman, yet she heard the voice of God and obeyed and now stands as one of the greatest pinnacles of light leading not only sisters of every race but brothers, men who need to know their worth, too! They can find solace in Bynum's words because she is experienced. She has been there, is there, and I dare say will be there leading until the day she dies! God bless you, Dr. Bynum. You are a light that does shineth forth out of darkness!

Then we have an angel on loan to men, women, and children in the personage of Ms. Yolanda Adams. I do not believe that any one woman has brought us into states of pure angelic hypnotic joy as this seraph of serene gospel spontaneity, this marvelous creature of elated joy. The infectious happiness and praise that happens when she ope's and she lets God wrap her in His spirit with that full straight line of perfect white teeth that seem to glow as she smiles or wails the words pour onto you and you are immersed in the presence of God Almighty. And if you never knew before, in the next moment you know and there is no doubt: "God is real!" I could speak of her many accomplishments. Being a mother of one that I pray will fill her spiritual shoes someday or at the very least exemplify her free and determined spirit to be alive, happy, free, and the friend of God that she is! On this path she leads the way.

When I start this kind of praise, I am overwhelmed in myself just to know that for some unknown reason I am allowed to be in the same family of people that they are. But I cannot stop for I would be amiss to not order my steps and control my pen just long enough to mention a women who walked, danced, pranced, and sang in the streets; made a name for herself with an old giant "boom box" on her shoulder; and dubbed herself "Queen" in the expressed image of the illustrious "Queen Latifah!" This lady took the adjective and made it the word for every young Black woman in her era could equal herself with . . . a word that made her (Queen Latifah) stand apart, but also told every Black female: it's time to stop following behind these Black guys and start leading these Black guys. And if you are right as a Black man, at the very least I'll walk by your side; but nonetheless, not anymore—we're better than that! We're queens, not chattel! From hip-hop to cinema, from there to the grandest award shows ever, from there to the

Red Carpet, she is what moving and shaking is all about. It's an honor to have watched her build and create an empire fit for "Queens!"

Yet what about the ordinary Black sister? What about our heavy and sweet brown sugar? We often times look at the hips, the shapes, the splendor in the way they walk and they carry. Yet what about "Miss Everyday Black American Woman?" Who will bring her into the sunlight of her glorious rising?

I look around and turn my head and then I find my head whipping back to the position from whence it came and the answer is only the obvious one—the only answer that can be. How can any woman embody the juices of a say "Naomi" or the quick jest of maybe "Whoopi" or the splendor of sensuality of a "Janet" and do it all from the stance of the most delicious full bodied, sweet as cream, sultry, and husky image nonetheless than our Mo-nique . . . yes, Mo-nique; the "Earthly", the "Beautiful", the "Real." The woman that is everything we want, desire, and need wrapped in the most voluptuous package God has ever attributed to anyone! Ladies, move over, Mo-nique has now arrived. She's here!"

If I may, there's only one way to say thanks ladies, and it has already been said in the poem penned by Langston Hughes, "Harlem Sweeties." I quote a line from this grand honor for Black women: "So if you want to know beauty's rainbow—sweet thrill stroll down luscious, delicious, fine sugar hill."

Langston Hughes can be seen and quoted in this poem as saying "cast your gems on this sepia thrill." Nuff said!

I'm 56 years old and at this stay all I can remember to say from days of youth is "power." "Power to the people; right on!" Left shoe, right foot, down on the farm, way out and upstairs! These seemingly meaningless words carried many a hippie and royal ethical radical through all of the days during Neo-Renaissance, and fed us with motivating truth that seemed to sprout different yet the same each day like toadstools from somewhere, from some great mind that had just received a revelation. No matter how drug-induced it was, drugs were the way to the fifth dimension and the portal to all of the Aquarian days that were so looked forward to!

Well, the days of Aquarius have come and gone. And that predominate peace was overshadowed by planes that were hijacked; planes that became guided missiles and the male instrument "erect" and hardened to plow into the Venus canal of American economic prominence!

Not only that, but we have an unpopular war (which we had unpopular wars between this one and the one greatest, that being Vietnam itself) and we, like the weary, have not been able as yet to rest!

The hippies and the radicals had the one thing in common: when they indulged in that "organic herb," they all seemed to conjure thoughts of violence even less. Maybe we should sell it by the pack! Five dollars per matchbox sure beats $10.00 a pack for "cancer sticks;" and they don't even promote peace. They just make your breath smell bad!

Anyway, these "Dimes" are in the stretch now and I hope that you guys by some process of osmosis will add your opinion to these very valuable pages.

It is very significant to recognize the beginning of this work!

If I remember correctly, I was investigating why we as Blacks and American whites and all other races have problems? Why white people find it necessary to hide us behind visible and invisible walls? Why we as Blacks allow it and why our familia is so <u>disarrayed?</u> The question arose also why we as Blacks mistreat our Nubian treasures? Why I myself find at times loin trouble with the same Nubians dancing delicately through my grey matter to points of uncontrolled sexual desire? Why the "B" word in reference to them? Why the "N" word in reference to us, by us?

Well being in the stretch, I stretch forth to answer all of this! The striving beast is still running, but now it is for a reason! I have control and he is running a race and running to win!

You see, I had not noticed that being and by the fog that there were other beasts striving along side mine—sometimes ahead, sometimes behind, sometimes side by side—but we are all running this race, this human race! Trying to make a hundred because 99½ just won't do! Realizing the race is not given to the swift nor to the strong but to him or "her" that endureth until the end!

Isaiah 40:31 says this: "But they that wait upon the Lord shall renew their strength; they shall mount up with wings as eagles; they shall run and not be weary; and they shall walk and not be faint."

Where does it come from? Well, the foundation of course for good and evil, for God says I create both!

If then the foundation being both good and evil, how then can it stand?

Come, let us reason together. God is the "artist" and with His brushes paints stars on the black backdrop of heaven! We see black as evil, or at least that is what we are taught: "that black is evil." Black-hearted, black-minded, black purpose, black hat of course "bad man!" Black man, evil man, bad man, no good man because he is "Black." When in truth, many Black men are "brown!" Then why that anomaly of prejudice?

The foundation like many other things is a springboard. The little stars can't shine in the day. Even though they are, "our eyes just don't perceive them." Without the black night, they seem to disappear and that one beauty is lost!

Yet we know that we will see them again. Practice or purpose? This is the question. Do we know they are there because we have seen them always in our conscious awareness? Or do we know they are there because of our dedicated purpose? In other words, "Do we just have faith?" How do we know?

Hebrews 11:1-40 now tells me a few things and I wonder if it is not dedicated purpose? Come, let us reason together:

<end excerpting>

Conscious awareness is probably our best friend. But there is some thing "faith" superiority!

My Bible tells me that there is something called "the sphere of faith." "That being, scribe . . ." that being this now faith is the substance of things hoped, the evidence of things not seen.

This is why we stand and gaze into the night sky waiting for blackness to unveil its most delightful protrudence in the fare of the "evening star!"

It is said that "by it the elders obtained a good report." I only find this relevant in that we need foundationalization in our efforts to report on our own faith! What better foundation then those that stood before us and gazed up into the sky to see their first glimpse of the first star; remembering the Star of David who led them to this place!

Speaking of the Star of David, we must remember by and through faith. We understand that the world's not just the world—we're framed by the Word of God, being in the expressed image of Jesus Christ spoke\; and so things which are seem were not made of things which to appear: Or better said, that things practiced nor by that which practice it. I know, I know; we could argue this all day and not get anywhere. But we are working in the arena of "dedicated purpose" as opposed to "practiced awareness!"

There are great recorded histories of "dedicated purpose." Such as by faith Abel offered unto God a more excellent sacrifice than Cain, by which he obtained witness that he was righteous. It of course caused him to lose his life, but God testifying of his gifts and by it he being dead yet spoke (speaketh).

Enoch. By faith Enoch was translated (removed bodily from his place on earth to heaven). That he showed not death and was not found because God had translated him: for his testimony that he pleased God.

Here being only two exploits of faith come full circle and claim all of the foundation, knowing that we need evil to see and understand good until all be good, and we need blackness to appreciate light. Not that all appreciate light, for many prefer the darkness, for their deeds are dark, evil, and black. Though we know the contrast is necessary, for us to appreciate the foundation of all things, ultimately "practiced awareness" becomes and truly is "dedicated purpose." Because in those instances, and many millions more each day, it's the dedication to the "substance of things hoped for and the evidence of things unseen." And the truth that we stand, gaze up, and live on a rock that stands a beautiful turquoise out of the heavens that we did not make nor can we make that makes us so complete and so magnificently important. It is this that allows us to forget. Like he stars we gaze at, many of us are merely the ghost of history and it is up to the living to determine the future of the living and those that will live to insure they have a foundation to rest there pediments upon; to have a springboard to jump on and leap into space; to seek a room where we can ponder this thing called "faith" for now and always. For as lovely as light is, without our blackness, the whites would have had no backdrops to ride in upon, let alone a springboard to spring from!

For only a split second I tossed history into this tossed salad of what can be easily called metaphors; yet being metamorphic, even history needs a foundation and I know without a shadow of doubt where that foundation is found!

For in Romans in the New Testament we can find in Chapter 7 these words:

V. 1: Know ye not brethren (for I speak to them that know the law) how that the law hath dominion over a man as long as he liveth?

<end excerpting>

It is in this that many of the men that were bound into slavery suffered such atrocities because it was written into the law—that same law that was preached by men: that other men that came to be called property of other men had no rights as men because the law claimed them to be less than men and, yes, even equated with monkeys and apes! Yes, and even today that vein of thought, though hidden deeply out of sight, is still engrained profoundly in many people in this the human society! Oh! You don't believe what I'm saying? There are doctors and aristocrats as well as theologians that secretly try to prove and create an equation that will prove our kinship to the Rhesus; although we as Blacks have proven time and time again of our superiority above the simple "Rhesus." It's odd, however, that there are many scientists trying to prove the human likeness to the chimpanzee or the chimpanzee's likeness to the human!

Above and beyond all of the precursors of confusion, it seems without law much of the prejudice experienced throughout would not have existed without the induction of certain preambles! At least in the suffering of the Black man amputated from the fatherland and mistreated as the Black society here in the "Red Skin's Motherland!" Yes, the Indians of this land, who of many tribes was and were almost wiped out, are the only true owners of this motherland! Yet by inducted law where they were dominant force, they are now substantially forced to live on reservations or only in areas common to the Indian populace, when in truth they should be the major governing bodies! Now that you think of it, don't you agree? After all, it's only American, now isn't it?

But what about you and me? We know the Indians are indigenous to this great land, but what about us transplants? Whether forced to be here or not, we are all transplants! This great melting pot of ideas, religious beliefs, and strategies; the only thing we can truly hold as a "common" is our hope of the American dream: "get rich" and do as quickly as possible! Thus the reason for the so many laws that allow some, disallow others, and give others for all their lives not even a glimpse of the "golden ring" or, okay, the "brass ring" in many cases, there are some of us that until today even here in America that don't even know what the American dream is or even that such a thing exists!

There are still far too many Black men that are born into poverty in this great land of opportunity, live, walk, talk, get hooked, catch diseases, give babies, and, as women have babies, get beaten of themselves; the enforcers of the laws (that many of them had no hand in creating) get hungry, turn to prostitution, become derelicts, live out their lives on the streets, beat their wives, and screw too much without consideration of overpopulation of a race of brothers and sisters that no race of people seem to care about, who have a minority that reach some stratosphere, and in truth don't reach back! Though many do, it is just not enough; and the laws say we cannot nor will we ever in mass do so!

The foundation is lain, and lain so that it reciprocates and continues to deny these little ones their rights to humanity! When I say "little," I mean it in the same arena as the Bible uses the phrase: "helpless people" and "hopeless people."

I find myself looking at those paintings hanging on the wall in front of me. And I am reminded by the "painter of lights" that God is all powerful—Kinkade is truly one of the angels God has set amongst men to express his tumultuous flinging of space and time while at the same time his quiet and peaceful serenity. The light of flashing and roaring storms and the quiet peace of a light shining in the dale from a country church—all one God, and indeed the exemplified truth that the storm will destroy—not maybe, if, and, or but—it will destroy. Yet when it is over, Ah!, when it is over, that smell of peace after great anger, the last drop, drop from what is left standing still, reminds us that we are blessed and not cursed. For truly if we were cursed, then where would the blessing?

"Scribe, you said all that to say what?" No matter what we are—Black, brown, blue, Jew or Gentile—God has made each of us all! Though the foundation that we have been taught to perceive lies, when we reach the quick, it's God . . . all God and nothing else!

If the Black is ever to reach his point of glory, we then have to reach down and pick up the Christian flag that race after race (particularly here in America) has dropped or purposely thrown down and wave it proudly and truthfully knowing we are on the right track and bravely march on! Oh, I do not mean holding hands and moving down a street to some distant point on the horizon of history. We've already done that. We know who we are, and it is not the "N" word. It is a proud, successful, and ever-advancing people who are intelligent enough to hold what we have already in our hearts. And no matter if the rest of the world dismisses it, we will hold on to God's unchanging hand; for in this is the reality of survival for all men! I am not writing this because we are expected to be saints. Quite the contrary. I don't care what your vise is—whether it is smoking crack cocaine, drinking moonshine insatiably, smoking weed, looking at girly mags . . . my, my, my! . . . buying those DVD's with all that pumping and grinding, going to your computer and clicking on some website that will, can, and should make you puke, or all of the above. The trick to not going ballistic is knowing that you are—believe it or not . . . and even though a lot of ministers call it a cop out and say it is not the excuse—fool, "you are human!" I've never seen or heard of a Rhesus doing any of the above. I've never heard of a donkey doing any of the above. I've never even heard of a (even though they call us so) dog doing any of the above! Don't you know that these vises are committed to humanity and not of any particular race, creed, or national origin? And they are created by other human beings for the expressed purpose to get you hooked on this wee bit of hell for the expressed purpose of getting you to give them your money for more! Yet the preacher has the audacity to blame you for being stupid and shameful, sinful. Why? Because many of them have done the same thing! This is where the rubber meets the road! We are not perfect—no man, no woman. And it is not mentioned about the girls getting together and just having fun "watching John Long" do what he does best: "bang that thang!" How they squeal with joy and tell each other what they would do with that "thang" if they were there! I know you must be flushed in your face by now, but don't feel alone. There are literally millions of women who buy into that stuff every day. That's why they make it. That's why they can sell it. Remember, it is only unacceptable when it is not called "adult sexual health tides." If they call it "porno," don't miss church this up and coming Sunday. You need the Lord and you need it bad! And men, if you are hooked on computer porn, you need to go to church! Get away from it fast as you can! Ms. Blue may make you blue, but don't let your juices send you to hell! In other words, from an old song of the 70's, "Don't let your wheels drive you crazy!"

"Now, now, scribe, how do you know of such things?" Well first of all, I may ask you, "How do you know of such things?" Then I would say, "I've been where you've been. I've done what you've done. I know the highs, the lows, and that puking dislike, self-hatred, and the helpless return to it time and time again!" You know what I mean. You've been there and maybe you are there right now! You stinker! The only difference in you and I is I know of whom I belong. And no matter the difficulty, I know that God sent His only, only Son to pull me out of <u>quagmire</u> just like this. For you see, there is no sin that Jesus is not acquainted with!

Want me to prove it? Whether you believe in God or not, it is always wise to know your Bible.

Isaiah Chapter 53, Verses 3-6 says these words about Jesus the Christ:

Verse 3: "He is despised and rejected of men . . ."

We know that this is true, and every time we have a storm and life is lost with everything destroyed, many of despise Him more and we can't understand why God would do that to us. Let's continue:

"A man of sorrows and acquainted with grief."

And we hid as it were our faces from him; he was despised and we esteemed him not.

Verse 4: "Surely he hath borne our griefs and carried our sorrows; yet we did esteem him stricken, smitten of God and afflicted."

Verse 5: "But he was wounded for our transgressions, he was bruised for our iniquities: the chastisement of our peace was upon him, and with his stripes we are healed."

Verse 6: "All we . . ." ["All we"—not one, not some—"all we"] ". . . like sheep have gone astray. We have turned every one to his own way. And the Lord hath laid on him the iniquity of us all!"

<end excerpting>

This point does not end exclaimed, but I feel it needs it! Yet we think the basic sins are so great. Yes, I said the basic sins. "What do you mean, scribe" If there was some kind of poll taken that could be trusted, it would shock America and the world to know how many people—not per capita but individuals—who have committed the aforementioned vises and think nothing of it. It would threaten to tear down modern Christianity to know how many so-called church goers imbibe in the same. And it would break the bank if not for the sacrifice of the Lord Jesus Christ to realize how many Christian leaders there are that do the same!

Am I devout? Yes. Do I trust? Yes. Do I sin? Yes. Have I committed such? Yes. Am I ashamed? Yes. How do I abide?

These questions are pertinent. Because I am "devout"—only meaning that I am devout to God and not to Satan! How can you be such a hypocrite? I'm not. Remember in the beginning of this conversation I spoke of being human. Well I am. If nothing else, I am "all human!" If we could encapsulate it, being human is all of the above—sins, joy, tears, pain!

It's not because we are human that we can escape these things. It is because we are human that we are trapped! Yet as Black men and women, and as Christian church goers, and as "sinners" . . .

"What did you say, scribe?"

I said "sinners." For the Bible in which we cling so tightly and of which our younger generation and many of the old are relinquishing in more and more at an alarming rate of time and speed, "tells us" we have all sinned and come short of the Glory of God! Our sins may not be the same sins; but according to the Word, "there is no big sin nor little . . . sin is sin!"

We as Blacks need to let up and give each other a chance to survive, to live "with our rights and wrongs, our mistakes, sins, good and bad." After all, we are not the Rhesus monkey; we are human!

Realize that the Bible even gives a great deal of slack to us. Chapter 54 of Isaiah at Verse 4 says: "Fear not . . ."

And the reason we do hide so much in the race is because we do fear. Fear this, fear that, fear old wives' tales—"Well, Mama did it this way and Papa did it that way. And if it was good enough for them, it's good enough for us." Yet we are trying to hold on to the old ways while trying to assimilate to modern society. No wonder we are snuckered and confused at where we belong!

Verse 4: "Fear not, for thou shalt not be ashamed; neither be thou confounded [or confused], for thou shalt not be put to shame. For thou shalt forget the shame of thy youth and shalt not remember the reproach [or mockery] of they widowhood anymore."

<end excerpting>

Just to add, you can be married and understand what it feels like to be a widow! On this I speak with authority of the experience, though my wife and myself are much more close these days than we've been in years! The years have provided and the years will provide for us . . . all is well! Remember the Rhesus loves to play with the tree boa and most of the time he ends up in the tree boa's belly! Let's not be stupid; let's not be so critical of each other. If God can forgive, why can't we? Being a brother is more than the right move with our hand shakes; even the whites have learned to emulate these. Where is our power now? Don't you know that's why we have so little respect of the races? I know the hip-hoppers, the rappers, and such have really excelled. But what about "Joe Blow Everyday Black Guy?" You see them on the street everywhere, walking along the road with a bag of brew or a lady carrying a babe and two walking along side!

I don't know about you, "Joe Blow Black Guy." I'm tired of generation after generation being born, living, and dying in exactly the same way as former generations. We can do better than that! We just can!

I'm not critical of our lack of effort, for God only knows we try. But the system is designed to keep us from ascending! Yet all other races can come to this country where we have been for three centuries, start businesses, become moguls, and own whole blocks on which we live and we end up buying from them, giving our money to people who came last and are now first! "In your face!" Is there any wonder we are the least respected? Don't you know, Black people, that when they look at an upward ascending Black, they look at him playing ball, making music, or dancing? Not much different than when we were in the twenties. We are not commercialized as the people we can be or we are! They don't see us as corporate; they don't see us as inventors, doctors, or pilots, although we exist as such. The economy does not revolved around us. It's not because there is not enough. It's because, for one thing, we are busy making our own and we are not enough in number to reach back!

If we reach, it's like crabs in a crab basket—one tries to climb out and the others reach up, grab hold, and pull the upward climber back into the basket, and we all go into the pot!

I spoke of new races coming into the nation. They are upward ascending because they sacrifice for each other! I know there are laws in place that give them a boost, but it's mainly because they boost each other. We should, too! We can; we just don't. It's time we did!

I'm tired for one of seeing us folks sucking hind tit! Let's look up the Blacks who are trying; let's look them up on purpose. Let's put something like money into that cruise. Let's incorporate. Let's own real estate, buy out these small stores, and build malls. We have the money! If we would just loan each other the money at a lower fixed rate than these money stores do, and reinvest it into the upward ascending Blacks at a return, and then place ourselves as a block on the stock market, we could start to own some of America instead of renting what we own! They rode in on our backs and they are still seated nicely there! Wake up! We strain at a gnat and swallow a camel! Believe me, there are going to be more and more camels for us to smoke and swallow as the months wear on . . . not years, months . . . time's up! Black man, Black woman, time's up! Wake up!

As I search for two nickels to rub together, *The Days of the Three Dimes* takes aim on some very diversified and difficult subjects!

Yes, Black man, Black woman, time is up! A thwart everything else, as I look even at the geological and geographical world we live in, it almost makes me wonder, "What is the use?" It also makes me ask the question, "How many others of us are asking the same questions maybe?" Finding the answer somewhere in their subconscious, realizing that with the earth gone berserk with these remembered climate changes. Indeed, what is the use of trying? Why not just enjoy today because tomorrow is not promised—to me, to them, or anyone else?

When I look at that square—or should I say that cubicle joy stick called "computer" or its cousin the television—and see every day the signs of the times, I wonder!

I think it's been coming on for some time but not at such a rapid pace; never like today. I am 56 years young or old (depending on when you were born), and I have never seen nor heard of the natural changes of this physical earth taking place at this speed before! I think my warning bells went off when I first heard of the poisonous copperhead snake mix breeding with the otherwise harmless black snake in West, by-God, Virginia and they're denning together! This is a natural no-no! It's kind of like saying lions are breeding with zebras on the Serengeti of Africa! Get my meaning? That's how unnatural it is!

The old folks blamed the climate changes on the "space shots" of the late sixties. How the weather was and is so different. Of course, this is relative to the years in which you were born. To the modern child—say ones that were born in 1999—the oddity of the weather is only something you hear about from the old people. O yeah, by the way, the quiet, un-gentle old people are those born only 5½ decades ago. Uggh, uggh! O yeah, that's you and me! Seems odd to hear myself referred to as an "old person." Why, I remember the twist and Chubby Checker! Who? O well, I was young and they were old—those that could not figure out what all that wiggling was about!

I wonder, do dances still have names? "All right, scribe, reel this beast in." You may not be able to make it stop, but maybe you can kind of determine it's direction!

Today is July 24th, 2007, and I was just looking back over the last three years alone. Correct me if I am wrong, but on two separate and unlike continents there has been as many tsunamis as there have been years! Do you know what the heck I am saying? Now today I was looking at that "cubicle joy stick" or my computer, and Europe's Thymes has overflowed its banks and more torrential rainfalls are expected before it subsides!

We haven't had time to put that Katrina in a dark place in our heads so we can live on yet! We are still seeing displaced Blacks along the Gulf Coast, and for many of them, life will never be the same no matter how many FEMA trailers are in place just waiting for another blow! All we can do is hope this hurricane season will spare these people from any more "insult to injury" by the hand of nature. Notice I did not say by the Hand of God?

It appears that as God-fearing people we are too quick to say God does these things to us. But let me tell you, Satan has his time on earth. And if there is an entity that despises man, it is good ole "Slew Foot" himself!

It's just like the ole liar to make sure his arch enemy gets all the blame for this kind of massive destruction. Yet through it all, I am gladdened and my heart and spirit are strengthened to know that the people of "Orleans" and those all along the Gulf Coast pulled together under the Banner of God and not Satan in "Pandora's Box" . . . one thing left: "Hope!"

That reverberant cry of the signs of the times seems to be coming more from laymen as well as preachers today. In truth, the signs are all around us. Wars and rumors of wars. It seems as though we can't displace one war before another has started, and indeed in today's times, wars don't wait to end before another starts. For as it goes, another is already in effect affecting all of us that hear and perceive it!

Earthquakes in diverse places from India to the Philippines, to the China Sea, to Japan, to parts of and inclusive of Asia, which houses much of Africa!

Famines and hunger, starvation such as this earth has never seen—Darfur, Sudan, Nigeria, Kenya, China Basin, Olonqapo P.I., Mexico, the back streets and ghettos of almost any American city! America? Yes, even in the land of plenty, the old and the young starve to death!

"So, scribe, we know all of this. We hear it every day on the news!" Yes, we hear it so much until it goes through our brains like water through a sieve. And I believe that we have heard so long until we have become so callous and expectant of it, until we don't realize that we are close enough that we as individuals may be next in line! Black man, Black woman, the Word says, "It is nigh and is even knocking upon our doors!"

When I speak of nigh upon the door, I would be amiss, even though the country and the world knows by now and I am sure some of the more wealthy are counting their losses and I am sure some of the lesser are counting the purpose of the life they had and lost in just one day as the "Dow" hit the negative today at 300 points. I wonder if there will be any corpses found in the morning that are a direct result of said same? Though not an exact "Black Friday," it was a rather morose Thursday, the 26th day of July . . . as I had predicted it would be. But who listens to the commoner, especially when the commoner is a Nigger? Oh, I forgot, we are not supposed to use the "N" word anymore! Yet Ford did pretty good and so did the maintenance industry. You know, the cleaning folk! Oddly, both are held up by many Black men and women. Seems we're good with our hands! Ha! Ha! Ha! It's a good thing, too, that we have pretty good brains as well!

Yet even though it feels good, enough is enough. And I'm not sitting at this table to gloat. Oh, you don't believe me?

These "Dimes!" As the beast rages on, his black flanks foaming in the moonlight, I begin to look at myself as a scribe. And I ask myself, "What is the measure of a good writer?" What's the difference between lousy, good, excellent, or greatness? When and what one word changes lousy writing into greatness? The reason I ask this question is because I do not believe it lies in the many words. All know the greatest quotes were not the many words, just the few; not the quantity, but the value of that one word.

Shakespeare once said, "Halleluiah, brother!" A great word made greater by the name of the man that spake it. Unfortunately, it's all a lie!

Then maybe a great writ lays in the profundity of it's truth. <u>Truth</u>. After all, the Bible is a great truth, even though there are many things in existence that point to many so-called "facts" that would displace it as such; and if one thing is not true, well unfortunately it's "<u>all a lie</u>!" Where do we draw the line between what we accept and what we know?

I know I woke up this morning, started on my way, and now it's night; and all I have to say is it was a great day because I am still alive to see it draw night, it's end! Hum! A lot of what I just said can be heard in just about any "good" Baptist church in the world. So does that make it rhetorical or just good ole Christianity?

If that's good ole Christ-like praise, then why is Christ not in our praise?

The root means square or the square means root is found based and grounded in the Word; and we are taught that the Word is Christ—not the fair-skinned, blonde haired guy; but a ruddy, rough, dark character of a man. The Bible says, "He was made so that none should desire him!" So we can't say that He won by His looks. In truth, the man was probably verging on ugly. Now what is truth? The truth is square means root and root means square gives exactly the same answer. But the one way is very easy to calculate while the other is very complex. Of course, we are not taught that in school; at least the Black kids are not! I wonder why?

The way I write and the way I think would almost lead you to believe that I am prejudice. But that little puzzler was resolved for me by what just happened to be a white woman from Idaho who happened to live and was raised in and around "Snake River" country, could pick the eye out of a cockroach with a .308 lever action Winchester, and was the best lover this Black guy ever had! "Damn, scribe! Scribe! You're Judas, the damned!" Well I may be the wandering Jew, but so is the flower!

Flower I may be, but don't begin to think that my name is "Petuli." I know I write fair prose and I can even put a poem together, but I prefer a 30.06 Winchester. And yes, lady, if you are reading this, I can at last hit a tin can with it!

Ha! Didn't think I'd learn, did ya? It may throw me down, I may run into a chain-link fence at the laundry mat, but you know I'm glad I got back up and got on board! Thanks, Alice; you're one of the best!

Well time and tide waits on no man, and the tear-jerking time is over. Back to this hole-ly writ!

I've found this striving beast of emotion to have a soul and more spirit than I had ever believed it to have. And even though my knees are locked, my thighs are beginning to ache me something awful; these branches are whipping my face "wetly" as time on the horizon is wearing away and a new day is rising like a grey long-haired ghost of a woman that died long ago. And not what you would expect, "as the wail of a new born child!" No, not at all. Not a babe, but the spirit of one that refuses to die. And let well enough alone! Almost Slick" like! Almost, almost. I couldn't say this if I had not buried that entity three decades ago in hallow, holy, and neutral ground where both the blue and the gray died, laid down their weapons, fell down in the blood-soaked mud, and cried. The same place where the war, that war said to end all wars, came to an end. And the Black man was set free to starve along the road! No more mansions, no farms, no cotton fields, no crops, no clothes—just set free!

Do you know what happens when you take the chain off a dog that has been tied in the same place all it's life? Do ya? Well, I'll tell you. It just sits there. It doesn't even know it's free. And for years, not months or days or weeks, it took years for the displaced African to know that he was free. And it took him even longer to know what freedom was. And it took the white until 2007 to begin to wonder what his freedom means—"let freedom ring" brothers and sisters of all races; "let freedom ring!"

Oh well, we were promised by Congress to be given by these United States of America 40 acres and a mule; and we ain't seen but one mule and that was the one that was about to die; and the same mule we was given by our white property owners for a lifetime of work share cropping; and we ain't seen the 40 acres yet! At least none that the United States of America has given us!

Hum! Some of you great Black math whizzes figure it out . . . do the math! What would the interest on 40 acres and the going price of one good mule have accumulated to now in 2007? And tell each other what we own! They may have rode in on our backs, but we'll hide out on their mule and it won't be a wagon pulling our coffin to the grave either!

Searching now is where I find myself astride this beast trying to find the road we were racing along through that pallid moonlight and fog!

Now it seems logic has turned into no more than a rocky path with briars all along that tear at my legs as I ride!

Finding two nickels to rub together is probably a lot easier than holding this striving beast on any kind of course and writing these "Dimes" is as difficult!

Writing is one thing; writing a truth is another. But writing a truth that someone really, really wants to read is pure praxeology of an art form lost to men of today.

"Well, scribe, if that is so, then how do you suppose to write these 'Dimes' accurately and without peradventure of the mistake of yes miscenscene?" The only answer I can give is that of a roadmap, even though metaphorically the animal has no clue as to where it is going nor in its headlong maddened rush does it care. But standing along the road watching and gingerly channel surfing, a brain that cries, "More, more, I know I need direction!" Thus I turn to a roadmap—ancient but universally accepted roadmap; a map that I have heard even the Koran keeps time with—the map "Torah!"

It's hard, however, to right the wrongs of the "Steatopygia" defined as "excessive development of fat on the buttocks, esp. of females, that is common among the Hottentots and some Negro people or Blacks or in other words, "She's got back!" Yes, it's hard to develop the miscenscene of this mind shot. But even that great King Solomon wrote the "Song of Solomon" to describe the allure of the stravage of a Black woman's beauty and her more significant assets—yes, this too the "Torah!"

Yet I believe without becoming too enmeshed in the polychromatic joy of this kind of woman (which is easy to do), we need to stick to the truth. Yet I'm not sure whether to lean toward the accepted truths such as the Torah . . . and I can't lean toward the Koran because I don't know it! Although I have from good authority, a Muslim acquaintance that I had spoken with, that the Koran the Torah mix and agree on many subjects! Though this being true, the women have a very greatly different role to play in the lives of the Muslim as opposed to the Christian. The polytheism of the Christian faith seems to allow more stravaging of the woman folk in life activities. Yet it was not so in the beginning; and indeed they were treated more like they are in the monotheistic religion. It's however a question to me why a religion or lifestyle that believes only in monotheism does not rely on the monogamous way of marital relationship?

"Well, scribe, you've opened a lot of cans and I'm afraid it is not beans found therein but oozing, slippery little worms; and the rocks are getting larger along the path." Uhmm, is that the smell of that poignant, salty ocean air? If it is it would almost be "poetic justice" since we started in this country by terror of day and night via the sea. Why not study the map and see if it will not take us back to the very brink of where it began? Let's watch our women, men, boys, and girls escape the "uhmm, maybe yes" the podozoization of one race by another, many nations by one demon . . . Satan himself!

Let's look at the Bible; yes, let's use the Hebrew Torah! A truth, the whole truth, "let it witness;" you be the judge.

Is there a Word from the Lord? Yes! In Jeremiah the 7th Chapter beginning at the 1st Verse:

Verse 1: "The word that came to Jeremiah from the Lord saying . . ."

Notice this word was reported to come from that all significant one "the Lord himself!"

Verse 2: "Stand in the gate of the Lord's house and proclaim there this word, and say, hear the word of the Lord, all ye of Judah that enter in at these gates to worship the Lord."

It's odd that Jeremiah was not sent out into the congregation of sinful men but to worshipers!

Verse 3: "This saith the Lord of host, the God of Israel, amend your ways and your doings, and I will cause you to dwell in this place."

What place is this? It would appear that it is a pleasant place because God does not prepare lowliness for his children, though these and I have flitted very close to the flame!

Verse 4: "Trust ye not in lying words, saying the temple of the Lord, the temple of the Lord are these."

<end excerpting>

Jesus Christ, who was preceded by the Prophet Jeremiah by many hundreds of years, said this, "When they say 'He is there; go not there to meet him; and when they say he is upon the mount, go not there; and when they say he is in the desert place, go not there to meet him; for the coming of the Son of Man shall be like the lightening flashing; where it cometh from this place and goeth hither, and no man knoweth from whence it comes or where it goeth; so shall it be with the coming of the Son of Man, which is Jesus the Christ!" The similarity of the temple makes me remember that Jesus spoke of his body and ours as the temple. Thus trust not in lying words saying the temple of the Lord, the temple of the Lord are these, for in the end of days many shall come saying I am he that you looked for—"lying tongues" all!

Since we have bonded with these boards called the Americas, we somehow have forgotten our horrible start!

"O scribe, not that; it's better just to forget!" All I can say "cliché" . . . "If you forget where you came from, you won't know where you are going. And, I might add, or how to get there!"

The roadmap or the Torah is trying to tell us not only a way to rise above our own self abasement, but also how to take hold of an oasis in a dry and tumultuous place; very much like the world we live in today!

Verse 5: "For if ye thoroughly amend your ways [change] and your doings, if ye thoroughly execute judgment between a man and his neighbor;"

Verse 6: "If ye oppress not the stranger, the fatherless, and the widow, and shed not innocent blood in this place, neither walk after other gods to your hurt;"

Verse 7: [Then this verse is completion.] "Then will I cause you to dwell in this place, in the land that I gave to your fathers, forever and ever."

The Bible speaks on this wise: "that judgment has come;" and I believe that it will come on all men. But if you can believe these dark sayings, which are truly "light," then understand that judgment doesn't begin in the street but as the Torah says, "that judgment must first begin at the House of God!" Not as you would expect at all!

Ah! This "Torah," this Word! It's too great to get over it, so wide you can't go around it, so deep you can't go under it. As a deacon friend of mine says, "You just have to come in through the door!" quote-unquote by Deacon John Andrew Hodge!

Some things are so obvious until we can be looking right at them and not see what we are looking at!

Chapter 8, Verse 6 says: "I hearkened and heard but they spake not aright; no <u>man</u> repented him of his wickedness saying, 'what have I done?'"

In other words, "I ain't done nothin' wrong!" As if this omni all things God were blind and backwards! Instead, everyone turned to his course as the horse rusheth into battle.

Which brings me back to my senses and my battle with this all pervasive striving beast rushing toward the ocean where we were vomited from and those horrid great hell houses afloat, "the slave ships!"

Verse 18: "When I would comfort myself against sorrow, my heart is faint in me."

Verse 19: "Behold the voice of the cry of my people because of them that dwell in a far country: is not the Lord of Zion, is not her king in her? Why have they provoked me to anger with their graven images and with strange vanities?"

Just like in the days of this book, as long as men do not see God, they will continue to do the very things that will bring his wrath upon us—that is, if you believe such. All I know is that I keep seeing the prophecy of the scriptures and the old writ coming to pass or "to be" every day that I live. And even I can't seem to get past "groinadle exercise" and, like the priest, I know what I see! Let alone invoking the spirit of Baal or Baalok for to praise!

Verse 20: "The harvest is past, the summer is ended, and we are not saved."

Now you have to rationalize that these times were before Jesus the Christ was born! If all had been accomplished, then that pointed to the time of the end. Where in God's name do we stand now? This book carries no small amount of references to our Black condition. Then it comes as no surprise that Verse 21 should read this way (of course I did not plan this, for the Bible is just too old):

Verse 21: "For the hurt of the daughter of my people am I hurt; 'I am black,' astonishment hath taken hold on me."

Verse 22: "Is there no balm in Gilead? Is there no physician there? Why then is not the health of the daughter of my people recovered? I put forth that there shall come a time that we will look for him and he shall not be found, that Great Physician, Jesus Christ."

In that day and in that time my hope is that all Black men, Black women, boys and girls will have found Him for themselves in their hearts, minds, and souls! Not on the electronic joy stick, not in the spotlight, but in quiet recognition of who we are and where we were derived! Black man, stand up. It's time to lead! Following behind is no longer acceptable. Where our spirits rest is up to us. They taught us garbage to blind us. What they didn't know was that "one man's garbage is another man's treasure!" Thank God we are still "makin' it!"

Chapter 10, Verse 21: "For the pastors are become brutish, and have not sought the Lord; therefore they shall not prosper and all their flocks shall be scattered."

Verse 22: "Behold, the noise of the bruit is come, and great commotion out on the north country to make the cities of Judah desolate and a den of dragons." [Keep an eye on North Korea, Black folk! Watch as well as pray!]

Verse 23: "O Lord, I know that the way of man is not in himself." [Thank God for this prophetic statement, for I would fight myself daily at my un-accomplishments.] It is not in man that walketh to direct his step.

Verse 24: "O Lord, correct me but with judgment not in thine anger, lest though bring me to nothing." [Thank God that "the steps of a righteous man are ordered by God." If it were not so, the weeping prophet could not have bore his time and these times that he saw in the future!]

Verse 25: "Pour out they fury upon the heathen that know thee not, and upon the families that call not on they name: for they have eaten up Jacob [which happens to be a forerunner] and devoured him, and consumed him, and have made his habitation desolate.

<end excerpting>

Now as far as we know, Jacob in this case is the forerunner of all sold into slavery and he believes in the one true God! If you believe such, say "Amen!"

It is said that the measure of a man is what he accomplishes in his lifetime. Yet I believe that the measure of a man or woman is what they accomplish in their belief system!

Therefore, you may begin to unravel now and stop asking yourself, "Why the preachment?" It was not supposed to be, but these measures in the Bible (believe it or not) are sometimes called poetry—that is the book of Jeremiah! This His measure; this our belief. It's here that our foundation is forged!

It is here that we became acceptable human beings, whereas before we were seen as apes! Our ability to articulate the scriptures was greater and more profound than any peoples before or since. It is this sense of spirit that made us whole, kept us sane, and made our lives worth living. As meager as it was, when we praised and praise God, we are rich!

I would be amiss not to preach just a little! Church was really the only true national treasure we had; and we must not for the sake of the modern world relinquish it!

The Days of the Three Dimes may not be like anything you've ever read before, but the significance of the writ is that it reminds us not to sit on our laurels as if this previous accomplishment was the laudanum for our ever-present pain!

You see, we have this permanent extensive sunburn and the world is always more aware of it than we are. Yes, it is true: "Black is beautiful." That's why so many white men from the very beginning in Africa to the slave huts and torture cabins to the Big House wanted and did perch ever so tightly between a Black woman's thighs and white women got a whole lot of Black men lynched because they were caught with them and hollered rape! Yes, they screamed "rape" and whites had an excuse for that inbred hatred of the dark man and hollered "rope!"

I guess looking up and down through the lives of us all, the thing that always makes me want to vomit is that it took so many—some big, some small—but so many white men to persecute and execute one Black man who had indeed done nothing wrong!

It goes back to the beginning of this book . . . we never had the nickels to rub together, and when we did have joy, it was often times that lump in our pants—too bad our brains, our common sense, headed south right along with it!

Even today we'll climb into bed, get a baby or Aids, call our Nubians the "B" word, and move on to the next one. God only knows, but I believe that many, not all, Black men think it is some kind of duty that they must perform for this society—getting one woman after another pregnant and leaving their children strewn along life labored paths with no arrows to point the directions or the reason why they are in this futile world!

Yes, we still need the church and God even more importantly than ever. Not just the Black, but every man!

Though I doubt it, if the consciousness of mankind is pricked, we may just still get that 40 acres and that damnable mule . . . and the interest as well!

In the meantime, I believe it starts with "one" and spreads like hot butter from one man to the other; from one family to the other. It's about family, not stragglers all alone in this world. And the ones that are alone, we must begin to realize this is family! Stop walling your eyes at one another; stop the gang fights; stop the alley knifing; stop shooting each other in the head. The Gestapo has already done enough of that for us and continues to do so. Sooo! Why don't we just <u>stop</u>!

Stop all at once and look at one another and our condition as a people—where we are, where we should be, and where we need to be as a <u>people</u> and as a race!

The reason Africa suffers so much is because we don't reflect on who they are, as family; and where we come from, as family; and truthfully our obligation to family! Yeah, you may say, "<u>they're over there</u> and I don't know nobody over there." But brother, they are you and they are us! What happens to them "will" happen to us!

Read *AT THE CRSS* on Amazon.com, the book; the biography may sound ludicrous, but what happens if it's real?

That statement was not a jump-off of some sort to just advertise another book, but it is another way to look at the downward spiral of our society. Take it for it's worth, nothing else!

The Days of the Three Dimes has been cooling (as a sort of metaphor) on the window sill of life. I've been, I must admit, on hiatus hoping that by breaking in the book, I can go in as a "word warrior" and win this contest of literalism and come out the top, with all of its multiplicity of word the top of the stack, the most honored pugilist!

The dawn has come and the ocean draws nearer; the giver of life on these shores for the Black man as with all of the melting pot of American people! This steed has slowed its pace as it runs through the sands. The sands in the hourglass of life run quickly out and pile ever so high on the bottom of the vessel like the bones of our ancestors who suffered and died here! Our people have been allowed to "pullulate" or to breed freely on these shores and surely this would signal our guarantee of survival. Yet with each successive birth, regardless of the race, creed, or national origin, no matter where in the world we are, the land mass, air, supplies for life shrink and threaten the very life we create. As Blacks, we now have a superior mentality, and along with that heightened level of the mental train comes a much greater obligation to ourselves as Americans and to our not-so-distant relatives and ancestor, the Africans, to do all we can to sustain our world. "It starts by selective sex!"

I believe for us as "Blacks" we need to have good "public relations." It starts when we can take the eyes of the public off of our genitalia and onto our brains. This requires us to take our eyes off of our erogenous zone and into our mind! Until sex stops being the only thing we can crow about as our life success and becomes our reason for life itself, while starting to be infused with resounding respect of life that we create with one "man" parts and "woman" parts, at the same time taking a position of superior obligation for what we create as life and stop driving down the road in our new "Benz," "Jags," "Caddies" or whatever, watching some young Black woman dragging along behind her two, three, and sometimes four children that some nappy Nigga has filled her up with and left behind, we need to stop and clean up our mess! Yes, stop and take responsibility for what we do and for what we have done! Instead of using the "B" word and subordinating our women folk and leaving them behind to suffer welfare, food stamps, and the mock of society for their children and themselves alone!

Why don't we have respect of the social system? As long as we do not fight our fears of becoming tied down and the mockery of our own brethren that "the hoe got us" tied down! We need to take pride in the fact that we are father and "pops," not street fools any longer!

Not only do we need to take pride in our children, we need to take pride in the women that carried those little babes for nine whole months and ended with their girlfriend, not you, standing there when she pressed down in pain to birth you a new life and a continuation of what you are—why I don't know—for future generations to come! There are just too many Black men that do this. And as long as we do, society will never respect us as a people. I don't care how much hip-hop we accomplish, the bling, the drugs, the basketball, the football . . . and our balls will hang there for the system to take pot-shots at because we don't stand up and protect our own. Dig? The striving beast moves on as I astride to hold; but now I am riding, not holding, for dear life; for now I am one with the creature and its name is "life!"

Line upon line, page upon page, it seems like that what I am doing is taking out the whip and acting like "Ober Seer," not giving us credit for the great works we have already performed!

Yet at this juncture it's not about what we have done—no more than we can take back Aids after we have induced it into our beautiful women, just to have them die by the thousands and give HIV to their newborn. Again not about what we have done, but what we can do about the derogatory, deprived creatures we have made them and subsequently ourselves by our un-thought, beforehand actions.

Now there are some mighty good brothers in this country and, yes, around this world; but I'm not talking about them. But I would be amiss if I did not digress and speak of the right "Mr. Brother!" I call him "Mr." because he does deserve all of the honor he can get—from me and everyone else!

He is the Black man who is willing to risk being called a fool and sometimes if by surprisingly the very one he has rescued; that being the Black woman with somebody else's kids! Yeah, she has the audacity to call this hard-working, loving, and kind man a fool, to say "he is my slave"—damn fool!

I have heralded Black women up to this point, but just like everything else, there can be always a bad apple in the barrel that spoils it for the rest. And sometimes with their mouth open like the "avenue to hell," spoils the rest and their chance for success over the more subordinate white woman. You might say men get tired of that mouthing off all the time! If there is a worse shrew, I don't know how or where you will find her than the shrewish Black woman! Walking, talking, and riding life—they are witches of the worse sort!

Any Black man who can and will stand in place as a husband and father for the absentee sire and consort of a woman with no one; "deserves honor!" He should experience praise every day by the children and the maid, not slander!

I find the brother one of the most interesting species of humans upon this earth. He can fight, he can relinquish his hold on his part of this society by falling into drug-induced stupors, he can be the greatest father, and he can put on his wife beater shirt and beat the hell out of some of the most beautiful creatures God ever created—spirit, mind, heart, and soul—just to maintain his sense of masculinity! It's so much of a shame when a 200 pound man beats a woman weighing 95 to 120 pounds senseless just to prove how much of a man he is. The brother is not the only race of men that do this. Many men of many cultures find this some sort of necessity. Why, I don't know.

Yet these men can sing the blues from the gut out; play an instrument until it cries! Not all men are devils. Not all women are angels. The truth is, these "Dimes" are searching for the middle ground—a place where we can all exist and subsist as one people, not striving beasts in a too cold world!

We are one on a planet that is already too small and "there just ain't no place to go!" When will we learn that time and geographical distance are far too short to meander on the edge all the time?

The conscious reality of men and women in 2007 is that we are hanging on like the picture of the kitten on the rope! I keep getting the sickening feeling that this world we live in and the higher powers are looking for the people who are more expendable than others. And the shame of it all is those that we're behind the eight ball in the beginning of this modern world; still are! It doesn't matter if they come out of Africa, they are still the most likely not to succeed by somebody's score sheet. And it doesn't matter whether they are starving in Darfur or thriving in Manhattan, if the world had to choose who would lose, it would be the greatest athletes that exist—the Black man and his brood!

In other words, we don't have time to work for someone else anymore. We don't have time to mistreat our women, our families; we don't have time to be hooked on the crack pipe. Because, baby, you'll be sitting somewhere in a drug-induced euphoric stupor and someone will point a weapon and you won't have time even to pray a prayer of repentance for the ignorant things that all men—not gender but sex—have a tendency to do! You see, we are not the only ones that make mistakes. We are just more likely to be accused of making that mistake!

"Well, scribe, powerful words; but where are you going with this?"

It's just that while fighting this striving beast, it seemed a lot easier to just do all I could to hold on; and the miles that passed under its hooves did not affect me because I was too busy staying alive. Now I'm not fighting the creature called "life" anymore. I'm just riding and flowing with the movement. But somehow its harder because I know that "life" will stop somewhere along the road and I need so very much to ride on. Yet I know "life" must end its journey, and I must dismount at the end of this arduous mile where every seraph and spirit, every angelic mute being stands looking, watching his mane blowing violently in the passing wind. This creature moving on and beyond every living and passing thing with speed which defies normal motion and the sand of time continues to sift away. Yes, this is my conundrum: to live astride "life" seeing it all passing too quickly by. Maybe not to have lived at all!

"Yes, scribe, this could be a conundrum of thought; but 'The Days of the Three Dimes' is not distinctly about you." It is about us as a viable culture within this melting pot called the United States and, yes, even about our upward ascension or the lack of, at least in reference to our time spent here! It is trying to tell us about putting away our witchery and our witchcraft, our beads and boards; and where we lack in our onward march toward the future, give what it may, give all that we have toward makin' it!

It's true in the side-by-side true analysis with other cultures that seem to have sprang up here, we don't have two nickels to rub together; though in reality we should own much of this country and its wealth . . . but we don't! There is a miniscule group called Black "millionaires" and an even fewer, single to double digit "billionaires!" This is not acceptable. There should be thousands if not hundreds of thousands who are millionaires! "O yea! Right, scribe!" How are we supposed to get past the government that takes from the poor Black in the form of taxes and made-up tariffs then turns and gives our money in forms of "perks" to foreigners who still hold that they believe in the United States but still hold allegiance to their own country, which just happens to be a foreign country that by necessity they still love?!

It's only natural that they would . . . everything that they represent is in their homeland, and rightly so. They (not like us) hold on to the ancient things that make them who and what they are! I don't know if this is our trouble or not—is that we are a displaced people. If it is, we need to go and gather the bones of our ancestors and give them proper burials instead of dismissing them as a foreign people "over there!"

We are the sum of what they are, and they are the root of where we came from and what we are! I note that on high feast days there is not disconnection by other cultures, but they wave the flag of the country from whence they hailed and honor their fathers, their saints, their gods, and mothers! It's all done on cultural days in parks and blocked off streets where they cook the foods and drink the drinks of their land. And the white American makes room for such activities and flock to them, even dressing in the garb of the culture and of the days. We in a small way do this, but it should be universal and not disjointed. We need a day of self-recognition of where we came from and whom we belong while finding out who we really, really are so that we can hold high feast days and know exactly why we are doing it. It is our right and our liberty, but we are too lackadaisical, "lazy." And because we are, we give all the other cultures room to make us "Black people" a "gazing stock!"

We need to stop being the "lackey" of everybody's culture!

We have the need for a ministry and ministers, not the ministers of the "Protestant" religion nor "Neo-Latin Catholicism," but warriors who will preach and cry, "Let my people go and find out where we came from," so that we will know in which direction we are truly heading! Ministers who are not preaching some new religion, but showing us why we cling to this one here. It is not only the religion of Christ we cling to here, but indeed the religion of the American "Pie in the Sky" . . . "Dollars, Get It All" religion! We practice the religion of the capitalist! When you cut away all of the layers and liars, this is where you will find us! Bowing at the feet of a mammon, the god of greed, the god of a material filthy and infested wound infected and fed upon by the flies of a society where "dog eat dog" is the accepted norm! We as a culture and proud, beautiful, becoming more beautiful, and desired people need to stop, step back a pace, and look over the ledge where we are standing, knowing that there is no place to go but back home! Home to our fatherland and motherland! I know we have sank our roots deep in American soil but, baby, it's just dirt. And when a plant is planted in dirt that has no nutrients—being just dirt—it cannot and will not grow. It may stay alive, but it will not thrive. Now doesn't that just remind us of us? We are alive, but we do not thrive!

It is partly because we do not connect with our ancestors and partly because the legal mafia, the government, has been playing the "shell game" with us for over 300 years . . . and we have let them!

I know we say we can't do anything with the government because it is the law and we have been taught to respect the law. No! No! Fear the laws! We as a people are under duress by the laws of this country, if indeed not under arrest by the laws of this country. We don't honor their laws; we are afraid of their laws. And well-placed fear is the springboard for the upward ascension of an oppressing and suppressing people to bounce from! It's no longer about prejudice; it's now about money and greed!

You wonder why we kill one another in the streets in gang wars? It's because we are taught by the media that money and greed are the way to the top. And again we take on the "crab basket syndrome"—that's why the Black man is always housed in one particular geographical region all over America! It's done, we think, because we prefer our own. Well, this is partly so. But just as true, we harbor together for strength! Yet I find that the people who watch us and are critical to other Black men and women who want to climb out of that crab basket are other poor Blacks that are going nowhere themselves! Thus we all suffer the hunger and lack of this suppressive society of America!

I've said it before . . . anyone of us that seem to be going somewhere, we need to get behind them and push them up and over the lip or edge of that crab basket. For as when we act as crabs and take the legs of the one escaping and all end in the boiling pot—conversely speaking, if we push them up and over by them holding on to us, we will be pulled up and over with them and shall all live! Not just live as a plant in plain dirt, but as a plant that has nutrition. And we then can say we have been planted by the "Rivers of Living Water" for we shall all flow together . . . "Life!"

Now we have power to give the laws of this country that cheat us and disfigure us by putting our young men away, locked away in prison cells, many of them to never know of freedom again. You know—out of sight, out of mind! We can now give the laws and the system that is purposely designed to block the Black while saying we have a dysgenic way or structure. In other words, we are detrimental to the hereditary qualities of stock; or that we are biologically defective or deficient! Taking a kind of "shockly" view of us as humans, giving them the go-ahead to dismember us by the hands of us as they have done in Darfur Sudan! Now the new word—give them "dyspepsia"—while coupling it with "dysentery!" In no certain terms, give them a mouthful that they will find hard to digest and then make them have a continuous bowel movement that threatens none stoppage! (I think this is appropriate since they have kicked the feces out of us ever since we have been Afro-Black America!)

We need this ministry so that we can look around and seek and find our own strengths; do away with our weaknesses and stop blaming other people for our failings. And, yes, I am not a knot in a log, I do know they stop and block us most of the time! Listen, don't you know that we are a powerful people—not only physically but also socially?

I watch some of these cooking shows and I must admit I really get upset that many of those recipes our grandmothers and great-great-grands created; yet we can't make any money off them! We need to learn to use what we have and we have a lot more than just music and muscle. We also have mentality and the things our "fores" gave us! Why do you think they passed them along? It's because they knew there is power in cultural recognition!

You say, "We don't have anything." Tell me, what do you know? What ever it is, therein lies your wealth!

What make up is your heart? Whatever it is, be it negative or positive, this will determine your success!

"All right, scribe, how can we succeed with the government's foot on top of us?" Well first of all you have to, as a people, stop being afraid to live somewhere other than just around an all-Black neighborhood. This will immediately destroy the wall built around us by cultural segregation; and then the world can look in and see our paltry existence! Remember, out of sight, out of mind. If they can't see us, they don't have to worry about cleaning up the mess in our culture that by necessity they have forced us to create—by close proximity! If you keep an animal penned up and never let it out, its waste byproducts will rise up around its legs and they will be standing and eating out of their own waste, also living in the same! This is why so many warriors died on the way from Africa just to have their bodies thrown over the side—no funeral, nothing to mark that passage, just an endless sea!

We have to draw world recognition to our plight; and this is not done by a bitchy moaning cry nor by protest marches! The best way to draw attention to ourselves is by a mass prison escape! Thousands of men, women, boys, and girls getting and receiving free education—not only about their culture, but about ours as well! We have a great and varied culture filled with truth and lore that we need to tap into.

Breaking out by having Black businesses hiring Black people. And when you get the job, work like a badger digging in to keep the job while always seeking out a way to become an employer yourselves! This tearing down of those invisible walls that stop us will draw a massive and world-sweeping recognition of the Black man and will cause more money to flow toward our cause! Why? Because we are the fundamental foundation, monetarily and systematically, for this country! That's why they have not killed and slaughtered us already—it's because if they expect to exist, they can't afford to!

When you ride down the street, look over at your white counterpart. Yes, just turn down your music and take a good look. Wonder to yourselves what they are really thinking about you? You know what the answer will be—so obvious it will shock the pure "H" out of you!

Now I am not writing a book on prejudice of any kind but, more importantly, a book on how and what we need to do as Black people for our own survival! Neither am I using some kind of scare tactics; but we do need to know that there is a very real threat made against the Black race all around the world while we dance, sing, and play!

Time to wake up, my people! Time to sleep is over. If we are to be treated as a real power and a real people, we need to break out of our government-made and self-made prison so that we can see the light of that promised new day!

You know we have been promised it for hundreds of years and have not seen it yet! I for one do not want to die just to see a promise made by men to my ancestors. The Promised Land is a place that cannot be inhabited by corruption; but indeed we must put on incorruption to inherit it. But this is promised by the perfected Christ, who is God! Not the promise of a better life promised by men! Though by living a proper balanced life spoken of by Christ, this life here can be also a rewarding one! Yet Proverbs puts the sluggard away for his or her laziness! We need to take a lesson from this and get up and shake ourselves and do what we are given the power to do—"Claim our victory until the victories are won!"

This book is neither judgment against my people, but I think more advocate—an advocate of our prowess however unused! Some are undoubtedly going to see me as some sort of Judas (at the very least a Judas-goat), but I stand in my own defense—I am neither!

I am 56 years old and all my life I have watched us make the same mistakes over and over again, almost as though we were addicted to failure. And I know, dog-gone-it, we are not!

People will look and say, "He does not give us credit for what we have already done!" Not so! But what I realize is that the ones who have succeeded are a miniscule minority that we as a failing majority ride in on the coattails of while "wishing I could do that!" Stop wishing. You can do anything that the successful Black has done. Believe in yourself and just do it! Make a plan, write it down, imagine it in your mind, make steps, and take steps . . . careful planning is the key! Take your steps and before long the broken majority will have become the healed successful and lucrative majority and the successful minority will be no more. For we will all—maybe on different levels—but we will all be the success stories one behind the other until our very presence will demand respect! Feels good, doesn't it? Well just wait until you are truly living it! Your dream is a dream no more but has become your every day reality!

"Scribe, that all sounds good but I have to be at work on the trash truck at 4:00 AM in the morning. What happens to me?" I know that you and possibly your family depend on your eight-hour day and your 40-hour week plus all the overtime you can get just to make it!

I understand, but I also know that while you are riding along on that trash truck, ideas come to your mind. Well these are not just ideas, but they are truly blessings in disguise! God is unlocking the chains that hold you in position by renewing your mind! Don't you know that just one of those ideas can make you a millionaire?

Take the idea and store it in your mind; don't tell anyone about it. When you get home, get yourself a pencil and piece of paper and try and draw your idea the best you can. Trash men are not broken despite the position they work in!

There is a company that takes raw ideas and makes them into working real world products. These companies are invention companies. They charge a small fee to invest their time and energy to bring your invention to the real world stage for sale and merchandising. This is where your money comes from. When you have free time, go to the library and ask them, not you, to look up invention promoting companies on the web and many times they will. There may be several; just pick one you like the best according to your pocketbook while remembering, "You get what you pay for," but also knowing that just because it costs a lot doesn't necessarily mean it's worth a lot!

Get their phone numbers and addresses. Call or write them. Make first contact. They will walk you through. Remember to call the BBB (Better Business Bureau) to see if they are reputable. You are now on your way!

Yes, on your way. This statement is a tap on the rear and go forward like encouragement to a child just learning to walk. We've been running for a long time . . . running for this or running for that. You know, the "go for" (gopher), trying to do everything for everybody; yet we have not learned to walk! Walk with our heads up and our minds set on our own goals to accomplish said same! I'd like to live long enough to see one thousand Black enterprises as Fortune 500 Companies in my lifetime!

The only way we can achieve that goal is backing. If the whites desire not to do that, then we as the average Black earner must consolidate our efforts and moves to promote ourselves in the business world so that we can be what we were meant to be and accepting nothing less. Not just achievers but "Black skin achievers"—self-motivated, self-foundationalized, self-funded, and a success story for the race of men!

"Scribe, you're dreamin'!" I know that and will continue to do so, for I do believe that the foundation for every reality has its roots in a dream. Dr. Martin Luther King, Jr. epitomized the value of having a dream! Not un-Christ-like, he gave his life for a dream. And because he suffered the bloodlust of white superiority thinking America, his bones lie in state; but each one is a key to unlock the doors of progress for young Black girls and boys who have no idea of what his dream truly meant in a time when we dared at the risk of our very lives to even have a dream of the magnitude of his! If we dreamed a dream of that strength, we were called "troublemakers, smart-ass Niggers" and the like. And there are people of our own race who said, "He's too smart for his own good," and turned their backs on a dreamer who dared see the light of freedom in the distance shining as a bright day star of hope.

Yet somehow the dreamer has always won out. Without him, many of the inventions pioneered by Blacks would not exist today. It serves us right to have nothing to hold to for the self-evident truth. You see, all we have to do is go to the library and look up Black inventors or inventions, old and new—and we won't even read. It's as though we are afraid of finding something useful. If you want to hide something from a Black, put it in a book!

112

"Scribe, scribe, that's being very critical!" Yes, it is being critical. But if shock treatment can work on a psychopath, it should work on the . . . hum, should I say this? Yeah, why not?—"the average Black!"

Now Mister, you tell us what the so-called "average Black" is!

Well we have to walk alike or you're not Black. You have to talk alike or you're not Black. We have to wear almost the same kind of clothes or you're not Black. Hum! If you don't coincide with the accepted Black norm, then you're not Black! I guess "the average Black" is just like all the other Blacks!

"Scribe, what the devil are you saying?" I took that stab at us and me because that is exactly how the rest of Americans see the Black race!

They don't understand ethnic and social identify; and this is because we have been behind the veil of inferiority for so very long. We are not inferior; we are superior. But until we have the guts to do what makes us as individuals feel good on any given day, we will remain "average Blacks," predictable and controllable, mind now . . . no way!

It's not a problem for the modern Black man to wear a plaid flannel shirt, jeans, cowboy boots, and, yes, a cowboy hat. What? Yeah, Black women started looking at the white cowboy persona as sexy and we hooked into it! Some even dare to act out and try riding horses; but it's all good, all good. Even the rind, "all good!"

You see, there was a time when the Black cowboy was not chique—it was a necessity, daily life! Yet we either did not know we could trace our roots there or we were afraid to believe my people were straw-chewing, tobacco-spitting, cowboy hat-wearing real heroes. Well yes, they were! We need to raise every flag we can convert with because we are everywhere for every time period for every people <u>forever</u>!!! Oh yes, and ah!—it's all good!

The time to strike is while the pen is hot! They have, this society has given us nothing but shame for our passage through life here. And we have nothing but the best things to be proud of! That's why all this cowboy stuff and many other things the urban Black man is doing seem so new and even fun!

It's because we were taught that either it wasn't cool to do such things or it wasn't Black or we had just forgotten with the passage of time that these were our people and our foundation, and, yes, we can choose to do this. It's all right to be a little different . . . why, it's even "attractive!" Black man, Black woman, lookin' good, Lawd! Every man in the universe knows what I'm talking about! For the first time the "little pinky" is giving ole "Black Snake Tim" some real competition!

It ain't Joe Blow Black Guy that we can call Jody anymore; not all by himself anywise, not any wise!

The question then arises as an old cliché, "What's it all about, Alphie?" When it comes to our women, the whites have almost gotten the Black in a clinch "arms locked moving around the ring of life" . . . all tied up!

So it comes down to this: we better get our act together and stop acting and give the sisters some much-deserved respect!

The Days of the Three Dimes has watched the hooves of striving beast pounding against flint rock, throwing sparks in every direction and setting afire the very stuff of mankind and womankind. It galloped through the snow and storm, beyond the mist, above mountain tops and into fog-filled valleys below. It fought me. I hung onto mane and bridle where there was none until the written word seemed to accept, by its own determinate will, the scaring of me of the virgin page.

You've seen us—our ladies and social order, our country and nation, our so-called place in the world picture and program—and out of it all, "The Dimes" has taken on the spirit of the Greek mask of that thing called "tragedy" and "comedy!" We who live here below the Mason-Dixon Line know all too well the tragedy of both! We have been talked about, laughed at, and talked down to; yet we have arisen and arrived!

Now the time has come for us to respect our women. Forget that awful "B" word. And sista's, you're guilty of using it too! Respect and polish our own social order. We don't need to infuse everyone else's into us; they just now are aware of the commercial bennie's of Blackness! Respect our world; something as simplistic as cleaning up the rubbish at our own homes. Yes, we may live in public housing, but it's home. Let's live like we walk, like we dress, like we talk—with pride and even arrogance in knowing we are the best. And by doing so, the world will beat a path to our doorway, for we will have the better "mousetrap!" The adage then comes true, "Create a better mousetrap and the world will beat a path to our doors!"

Then let's not forget of whose we are. We don't belong to other men. Matter of fact, we don't even belong to ourselves!

Verse 5: "There is one God and one mediator between God and men, the man, Christ Jesus;"

Verse 6: "Who gave himself a ransom for all to be testified in due time."

<end excerpting>

Of Chapter 2 of the First Epistle of Paul the Apostle to Timothy, "his son in the ministry."

Paul had an infirmity in his flesh. I have an infirmity in my flesh, and I guess this is the reason I can connect so well with Paul's word or epistles! No one knows what the illness was, but mine is clear: my infirmity is the "flesh!"

No, I am not a whoremonger and I am not into drugs or alcohol. I don't smoke "crack" or cigarettes. But there is a constant warring within me to fight against all of the above! I find that the flesh is always aware of the whispering behind its back; and is always telling itself, "I am not going to turn around and look." Yet the flesh in all its ways is governed by the material and the world in which it was born into. Therefore, no matter how hard it tries not to look, the head is constantly and ever-so-slowly turning in the direction of the world that says, "Look, look, look at me;" until the head and body—no matter how good your intentions—are completely adverse to where you were rooted and grounded, and you find yourself standing face to face with your bug-eyed temptations. And if not aware of God's power in the time of your temptation, you will find yourself suffering with the guilt of having gone astray!

I tell you, sin of omission is as guilty as sin of submission! My brothers and my sisters have in the street been so long until the sins of "commission" seem to them normal. And they don't fight Satan because to some he is a myth (just what he wants us all to think), and to some it feels so good to the flesh until we don't see why we should "plant our feet on higher ground!" Yes, my infirmity is not neglect of "self," but my sin is vanity in the form of applying too much time to "self!" You see, in order to grow, one must consider the other more than himself or esteem others higher than self. When you do this, you heal those and the world around you and thereby grow.

It's not our moral decay that gets us. God has already sent His Son to take care of that. It's our back-paddling from our moral obligations to others that destroys our "human!"

I don't want to <u>preach</u>, but our only "justificare" is Jesus. And because He justifies us with His blood and His testimony, we are then guiltless and we then receive salvation and are free in this present life and—if you believe such things—in the life that will come!

There is an importance in looking at all aspects of our existence: so that we don't have a lopsided view of life. There's more than one side to all geometric shapes and life is a georama of experiences that all together make us whole and fulfilled.

We need water but we also need air. With water alone, because we are not fish, we would drown. With only air, we would dry up and thirst to death. But without nutrition or food, neither water and/or air would suffice. But just like the triangle, a geometric form, we need all three to survive and be whole. As an observation, there are three sides to a triangle to make it complete. There are three sides or personalities to God to make Him complete: the Father, the Son, the Holy Spirit. But just like the triangle, even though there are three, all of the parts make one whole. And God is three in "one!" We as all things—though men be human, his highest order in creation—still sit at His feet. So look up . . . your redemption is drawing nigh! Soon we can say great old Auntie, Grandpa, and Grandma were right—"The top rail shall be on the bottom and the bottom rail will be on the top!" Can you lead your world? Are you ready to lead? Do you know what leadership is?

"Be as wise as a serpent and as harmless as a dove;" then the world will turn around. Be what God intended it to be and heal.

My wife has a pamphlet from Unity, 1901 NW Blue Parkway, Unity Village, MO 64065-0001, at <u>www.dailyword.org</u>. The pamphlet is called "Healing Thoughts."

I hope this is legal; I just want to do a quote of some of the words and thoughts therein. The title of the first thought is "God Loves Me." I did not write these, I simply quote since they are so sound:

"I have loved you with an everlasting love." Jeremiah 31:3
"Healing Thoughts" says:

Do I see myself as limited in some way? I may think of myself as being less than I should be. What a revelation I experience when I understand that God sees me as I was created to be: whole in every way, unbound by events or circumstances.

God loves me the way I am, for I am God's beloved child. Though I change from day to day, my Creator's love for me never changes nor is it withheld.

I feel God's love assuring me that I am never lost or alone. Even in the darkest of moments, God is with me. Turning my attention to God, I feel at peace, for I am in the presence of pure love.

God, my greatest supporter, has absolute faith in me—even if I seem to have none in myself. I soar to new heights on the wings of God's love.

End of quote and quotes: quoted from "Healing Thoughts," a Unity pamphlet.

The next quote from the Unity pamphlet is "God in Me."

"I will strengthen you, I will help you, I will uphold you with my victorious right hand." Isaiah 41:10

<end excerpting>

"Healing Thoughts" quotes:

I have turned to others in times of need, seeking the help and support I cannot seem to find in myself. I am grateful for friends and loved ones, of course, but only God will give me strength to surmount all difficulties. God's sustaining grace is powerful enough to transform feelings of weakness, loss, or loneliness into feelings of peace, strength, and serenity.

God is in the midst of me—a wise and loving friend. Wherever I am, my friend God is there. Wherever I go, my friend goes with me.

God's love sustains me through every experience. I am able to meet life with faith and courage.

"God is my wise and loving friend."

End of quote and quotes: quoted from "Healing Thoughts," a Unity pamphlet.

<end excerpting>

At the end of my own last report, I quoted a statement from the Bible. "Be as wise as a serpent and as harmless as a dove." These profound words from Unity begin to show us how. For indeed, we need a renewed mind that we may have a right spirit within us! Not like the plant that is planted in just dirt with no nutrients and cannot grow.

We become a thriving, growing, life-bearing proponent of life itself by living in the warming rays of God's nutritional love. A right spirit is renewed, created, and made in us, of us!

Let's see now, this striving beast called "Life" has at long last started to stride with arched neck and high held head. A beast of beauty at last, beauty and the beast are one thing—that "Life" and life with purpose and control!

The striving beast in the beginning just wanted to run, foaming a heated smoke and what looked like the fires of hell pouring from its flared nostrils. But now we know that no matter how much hell is poured into the world, the striving beast can be controlled. It is oh so good to know that the beast can be controlled, and we as men and women do not have to worry about the control of it. We just give it over to the highest power, the maker of life itself, that one "God" and Him in three alone!

When I began this book, I was holding on for dear life! Somewhere along the way, as bad as it can get, I find that all in all, it is life . . . and life is for the living and the alive! Jesus says, "Chose life not death." I over all have ridden us because I love us, and I don't want us as a people or a nation to be less than we are or were meant to be! What great celestial dye was cast upon the waters to say that men of the different sort were meant to strive against one another? I'd like to make a suggestion: Let's all get high!" You know, sloppy, crazy, slap-happy high; high, high, and even higher until we are in the presence of God Himself. Yes "high"—high on God. For through my searching, I find they gave us rubbish; but that rubbish turned out to be a great treasure!

I don't profess to know all of the great "secrets" involved in the true "knowledge," for much is hidden and much is lost. But I do know, out of it all, it is the best thing going—hands down! Over the period of my short 56 years in life, I've had an immense, immaculate revelation. I believe it is wise to share it with you and let you decide on your take of it. God said to me, "All of the religions of the world were given a small piece or amount of what I am really as a whole; and none of the great religions are perfected; and none have all of what I am! I am. Buddha, Brahman, nor Mohammed contain exclusively all that I am! It is and will be when all religions come together and make peace and share each one there part of what they know, "truly know" of Me that men will see Me as I really am: one true God for one—one man, "human kind,"—humanity will at last be one, and I will bless the whole earth as God of all men, the one true creator. My name is 'Tetra Tetragrammation' God!"

Now don't get me wrong. This is not some sort of blasphemous statement, for I am an ecclesiastic and I am bound by rules and higher laws. The name 'Tetra Tetragrammation' is one of the names of power given of God's men who seek to know the core of Him! Yet this is impossible. Men still seek to know Him. I find that the knowledge of God transcends all of the piety and the petty; it is an all-encompassing peace that contains within itself "love"—the true dynamo of God's power!

We as Black people have been affrighted into only seeking "sin" or "piety" as before God sees us He made us and seeks to have a personal relationship with each of us and that, too, all of us! I believe as it is wise to know that we have direct contact with our world as human. We thusly affect our world directly by our actions, whether it be war or praise! If this then is true, the negative actions of ours as well as the positive actions are rewards as well as punished merely by our activities in our world! The greater the mass, the greater the reward/punishment!

If we look through these glasses, we can then see a world undone by negative activity, and the great mass could produce an Armageddon or an euphoric heaven; and I believe that we can experience either very much alive! Then is hell real? Any place with descendent man and a destitute God where the creature is still desirous of the creator, him an absentee figure, for good cannot be recognized where evil abounds, even though it is not lost, is a place that can be called hell!

War is hell and we have been represented in every war America has proclaimed it fought for freedom; yet I know that our own freedom fight is a constant battle, a constant war! It seems that we are always on the front fighting to prove our worth or who and what we are. When will we just be allowed to "live?"

The church has been a sanctuary for the wayward traveler since its conception, and we have been like rolling stones since we were uprooted! No wonder that the church is our haven and we have embellished it in our own ecclesiological format from the inside out; first and foremost and utmost apparent in the way we praise! We as Black people lead the way in the voiced earthliness for the Black eclectic approach to his reach for heavenly or his ecstasy of thoughts of heavenly places!

It is also apparent that the African and the Afro-centric American has influenced the praise in a cross-cultural way, and it can be seen in almost every religious practice of the protestant search for the creator, whether the people be white or Black! This is the one place where we have a neutral ground!

Yet I am dismayed by the financial regime and the monetary approach to serving. I think because of the cost of religion rising exponentially with the costs that are produced by inflation, it begins to look like <u>God</u> is only in the reach of the well-off or the very rich, while the poor (who Jesus sent us to in the first place) have to take the crumbs and the leftovers of this society <u>figuratively</u> and literally!

Maybe this is the reason for the new church accepted by the young Black as well as many median age ones as well. The new church, "the world of music," being not new in itself has become a megalomania—the people having greater and greater desire for the grandiose performance—the need almost for the omnipotence in the performer—and pay for it we do and we will!

We find that more and more the young are leaving the church setting and heading for the street settings of hip-hop, rhythm and blues, jazz, and the like; even heavy metal is just under the level of being praised as God-like!

The church, realizing the competition, has allowed some of the purity of praise to flow and intermingle with rap-like gospel music and is not ashamed! What is surprising is the age brackets that seem to enjoy it, such as 40 and 50 years is unheard of. My question is this: a meliorate or are we losing sight of the real purpose of church as a gathering place to serve God as the church being ourselves or has it become a social mediumistic house of monetary gain having lost altogether the true ideal of a living God?

Then do we put God in the background, and do we take a meliorism approach to our worship? Is this a negative or positive edict? My answer is, "If God is excluded from it, it is not God." In other words, "If God ain't in it, it ain't God!"

I don't think we can afford to efface what treasures we have, even if it did start out like leftovers from a forced and forcing white society! This God we serve is real, and I believe we didn't have to come to America to find Him. He always did know where we were. And, yes, the God we praise in America is the same God we praised in Africa! I'm just glad my God is multilingual!

Because of the aforementioned standards, *The Days of the Three Dimes* stands strong; though I believe standing is not enough. This dialogue between you and this striving beast called "Life" must move. And in its arm clutching arm, hand touching hand, the sway alone as of wheat fields in the Kansas blowing wind creates a music, a rhythm of life, if you will, that we are all acquainted with, no matter your ethnocentric positioning in this great universe of men and women!

Our days of self-disapproval have to come to an end, represented in our casual use of the "N" word or "Nigger!"

The almost happy use of the word "B" or "B" word and bitch! A bitch is "a female vomiting, flea scratching, behind licking dog!" Our ladies—beautiful, bland, or ignorant of who and how precious they are, mainly because it has been hidden from them for so long—are women of the highest order, ladies of the grandest kind. And Black men, get it together—we have to be men! If our women are considered dogs, what does that make us? Just let some Joe Blow White Guy walk up to you and call you a dog . . . !

We have to stop standing as the profane. The lexicon defines this word as: "1. Not concerned with religions or religious purpose: secular. 2. Not holy because unconsecrated, impure, or defiled: unsanctified. 3. Serving to debase or defile what is holy: irreverent. 4. Not among the initiated (b) not possessing esoteric or expert knowledge—profanely (adv) profaneness!"

I believe the Black man has truly escaped because, although society has seen us and ours as all of the above, upon close observation, we are none of these! We are not the profane and never were. We are not heathen, although we are humans and I believe that at some point there are men who fall into this category. Yet who are we to judge any one? For by judging we become the profanity of life; the Bible says, "Judge not!"

Throughout this essay I've tried to be honest and to put down what I've seen and know, experienced or felt, knowing that I am no professional by any means! Leaning toward life as my resource and proof, I have written this "procedure" of our life and living. This is my examination of who we are, of who we have become, and, by viewing the national standards, this is also the way this country views us! That's why it is so important to give positive role play for the up and coming generations of children behind us. For in truth, we stand upon their shoulders and springboard into the future from their minds! It would seem that they depend on us, and in a way they do, at least to nourish them until they can nourish themselves. But the future of our race as an ethnocentric society, our future—if we are to survive—depends on them!

We then need to teach them right thoughts and right thinking processes; not fables (unless it is cultural remembrance), not myths. We don't need these anymore if we expect to grow and become real players on the world stage of humanity. Our children are our greatest asset, our greatest jewel, and our true "bling!"

This is why it is so important to stop taking advantage of our best repository of life, the Black woman. Not only is she precious, she is perfect; for out of her comes wailing, crying, screaming "futures" of our social order! We need to stop being our own "assassin" and start marrying the women who become pregnant with our babies so that these same babes can grow up knowing from whence they came, so that they will have some idea of where they are going. Do you feel me?

If the Black woman or any female is good enough to lay down with, they ought to be good enough to wed.

I ever get so tired of watching a young woman—not old, "young"—her life ruined, walking along some rocky, dusty road with one, two, or three chaps with no husband and the children with no father. This is not our beginning . . . it is our end!

This woman may even be the product herself of a fatherless, absentee father relationship by her mom and some man that she only knows by name, and many times not even that!

I myself have been subjected to this type of tyranny! Do you know what it's like to have other kids ask you "the question?" "What's your dad's name? Where do you live? Where does he work?" This dagger is red hot and is plunged into the depth of your core spirit. It can scar, and may very well be the reason why so many Blacks end up in prison in the first place. Besides the system step-by-step process of eliminating the Black population, this step-by-step of "isolation," "nurturing," and "spading" of the Black race has gone far enough. And no one can stop it but the Black himself. No one cares enough and the nation is blind of its own choice to the problem!

It's not just about the crimes we do commit; it's about the crime of self-abnegation we commit by omission of our wives and children that we initialize against self!

Before we let that itch overcome us and make the invasion of our Nubian queens okay, we need to stop and think of who and what our own obligation as men are to our social order. It is not about sustaining the race; it's about entertaining that "itch" and getting your "rocks" off! No matter the end result!

The invasion of the Black woman needs be and has to stop! This thing of . . . well, I didn't tell the "B" to do it, she wanted it just like I did . . . is only a cop out! You know as well as I do that we pride ourselves in our ability to "rap!" Then why do we "rap?" You know why. It's to get them "draws!" Come on, who are you trying to kid? Been there, done that, stopped that, and am writing this book about it because it has become an epidemic!

Rap maybe. Rap it up "defiantly." Consider the outcome of your actions, yes. Stand up, take charge, yes. "Be men!" If we want to claim any part of this world, it is imperative!

I'm not talking at you; I'm talking to you . . . and it's because I love you! We are a great people. If some can make it, we all can make it. But we have to stop depending on "ole slew foot" (the devil), which is this society! It will never let us get ahead. It will never make a way for us. We have to close ranks, come together, make our plans for success, and "go for it" as one great spearhead of effort! We have to stop trying to talk all at once and start talking one at a time, and teach ourselves how to listen, then good ideas can surface that we can use to promote our futures!

We, too, are a thinking people. Once we get rid of our "stinking thinking," we'll springboard to the top and nothing can stop us . . . nothing at all!

You can do it. I can do it. We can do it.

Life now is trotting along at a pace that is acceptable. The things along the way are no longer a blur, but I can see clearly now the fog and the mist as if I was riding along a path where only death was . . . is no more!

I can see everything at each side of me and in front of me. This great steed is alive and so am I!

One of the most jubilant sites I see is the Black woman—today a matriarch and a matrix of life, a procurer of fresh oil for our enlightenment and our enlargement!

One who rises early to trim her lamp and goeth forth to meet the Lord!

She enlists the services of her friends when her man is not around; raises her children alone without complaint or compromise!

She stands a shadow, a silent powerful wind, a breeze through a longing silhouette! She is the picture and the photographer! The maid and the mistress, the queen, the naïve, the jester, and the wise sage!

I "even" is to be caught it will be held in the aged and veined hand cupped gently around it as she does her grandchildren pulled so peacefully to her quiet breast, breast that gave suck to so many men, girls, and boys in a lifetime of effort to nourish and appease the devils of this life, that were turgid frothing waves of the sea!

She is beauty and beauty that is not beautiful; her nappy hair is wool and full of delight. How many ways can she prepare it? Can you count the stars in the sky just by looking? If you can, then you have seen her locks and know they came from that same nappy and substantial head!

Playing in puberty, her smell is that of the great forest loam; she is clover blooming after the rain!

Like joy, she is that which fills the head and heart with laughing as she steps high, trying to find her footing or womanhood!

She is a young woman, this Black star, this opulent breath that enters your nose when you stand close. Have you ever smelled virgin breath?

The rose just now open, displaying within its contour magic that defies the eye to follow each swirl; down, down, down into its middle soul!

Where is your beginning? Is there no end to the treats and gifts you hold within your bosom? Can I peek at just one?

Berries and dreams of running on sunlit days, watching your heated now black and brown, tan, joyous as we hold hands through buttercup fields!

If you have not that chance, think of living gold waving, settled close together as giggling girls just sharing a laugh and a secret that no one knows!

She has made me leave the room as women are talking, and I leaned close when she pulled me up close between her long dress covered legs to her ample breast to talk and tease!

Did she know the neighbor woman next door that I peeked further than I should at a place where her dress did slide upward; and my beating, tripping heart almost shot forth from my chest as I looked "a boy!" . . . did she know?

Humble and proud, tall and short of stature, mouth spread wide in the glorious songs that praise her God. Can she sing? Only the birds are quiet when she ope's!

Her songs don't talk of one thing, but life she implores—from waking to sleeping, her joy, her pain, her quiet agonies alone, and slaves her flesh exemplifies and her spirit even more!

Down on her knees, praying for peace or a piece of bread for her babies. She bakes a last cake, but instead of eating, gives to the prophet. Is this why her meal barrel never runs empty and her cruise of oil is always full?

I've seen her fight another woman for what is hers; balled fists like a man And I've seen her fight the devil "stand!"

Many songs are written for her and about her. Today, credit enough she is not given; so she stands and sings her own praise alone!

That song is not self-abasing but self-admonishing. Sometimes it's about her man and then her children, her song!

But when she is in rags and drugs have taken a toll, and she's just about ready to sell her soul, then the God we serve an angel sends to lift her by her needle and nail scared hands as she sleeps; but not eternally. The Black women is my wine, my brandy; the moon shines upon her naked full and ebony sweating breast, jutting to the sky . . . excitement—she is luscious to the eye!

Her Black skin just like satin and velvet; her eyes can make the seraphs cringe and molt away!

This is your loving child, too, and you cannot see the River "Niger" so quietly flowing through her veins from her head to the floor!

Sexy, sensual, at war in peace, our Joan, our Joy!

Maybe they are not part of this world at all but were pre-planted angels from heaven's doors! These given to men to employ; the making of the greatest nation in their dance, their thighs, and muscles proclaim them the more! More of you I need but invade you wrong I won't! I want you pure and that door back was not meant for me to enjoy!

Forgive my brethren . . . they take you as a toy. They do not know a queen is passing by. A food we are!

Can ashamed of her I be? Yes! When she opens her mouth and profanity pours, yes, and even more! My ladies, this ought not to be. Have you forgotten who and whose you are?

Yet I know when that Black sees red, look out! You're going to get cussed out and, if you are not careful, the hot grits and cast iron frying pan and even more "see this" (smack), kiss it! O my girls, women—more!

Like as a painter of light, a woman can bring a portrait of solemn peace. She is the truth and the keeper of our history—true!

Looking on her old patchwork scrapbooks, she sits and shares a past that is burning in her bosom of who we are. Is it not time to sing her song? Is it not time to stop leaving her alone?

I take the chance of being called a Judas for proclaiming her glory be!

Bet it known to white men, Blacks, all men, angels, and beasts, this Black is the finest of fine! I'm glad I sprang forth from between her legs, parted into a world unknown that I may end my life in her arms!

Black man is great, but if he will just look around, it was because of some or some man that came past a great woman that he is where he has come!

Don't think you don't have to pray for her longevity; we want her here always . . . this, her song!

The song that was just sang is to honor the woman who is rarely given a chance unless she is some famous, beautiful dancer, singer, or actress. But in truth, every woman of ours is the potential and the stuff of what they are made of; yet they are almost never proclaimed!

These "Dimes"—ah! These "Dimes" . . . I may never have but two nickels to rub together, but I am and we are rich because of where we come from.

The land where diamonds were found laying on top of the ground like mere sand stone, and where mountains reach to the sky; a place where the sound of the king of the jungle's roar is as common as a city dog's bark!

Where baobab trees so ancient they defy anyone's determination of their true age; where rivers flow so quietly and give no sign of the things there that can literally swallow a man alive; yet we have lived there always and always survived. Where the Black woman is queen, was queen, and served and birthed kings! This book of "Dimes" . . . a mere reflection and thanks to our women and our God that many of us as men have not forgotten, nor will we forget, because it is in the her heart to keep us! A "break" here is the flow!

Whose skin does gold look so natural lying against; who has teeth pure as driven snow and who can laugh and talk with no teeth at all making us laugh from wall to wall!

This writ is a plea; a wake-up call for you. It's a wake-up call for many because in truth, in this society, we can't live without rubbing elbows with somebody else's society, and I want every society to know the worth of our own! You can know very well who and what we are when you see our great athletes; and you can change the channel and as easily forget, still having the audacity to call us "Nigger." Who do you think you are? Who died and left God's throan room to you?

I'm not prejudice, but I do become—I'm going to use a word not normal for this context, and the word is—"self-righteous!" I know what it normally speaks of, but herein is my reasoning. We have bled. I have bled in many countries and many genre of life. And most of the time we have received no real lasting—and I say it again—lasting thanks for what we do! We are not always right, but when we are right, we are right!

The word "righteous" means to be in right order with God. But now—though I by no means equate us or me to being a god, even though God does call men "little god!"—we are right with our God and we are right with ourselves!

In this case, is it wrong . . . this examination of self-right attitude?

It is a case where we need to stop taking a wine bottle by the neck and choking it to death, beating our wives and our children, and by this ourselves. We are essentially good men, but this system has taught many of us that we cannot rise above our circumstances . . . and that is a lie! Selling drugs to our people and shooting our young down in the streets like dogs over some imagined demarcation line is unacceptable!

As bad as it is in New Orleans, the gangs and drug dealers there are so horrible, it makes the year of Katrina almost bland; for the fear it causes and the hearse that roll with our families inside! These men are so horrible that as bad as the police state is, I almost wish the military could take the bastards out and not bring them back and good riddance!

How do we ever expect to overcome and realize the real men and women that we really and truly are?!

Right now the people of the Gulf Coast are like candles blowing in the wind, having the chance of being snuffed out at any moment, and our precious government stands by twiddling their thumbs at us, pretending like they're doing all they can! Why, even the FEMA trailers themselves are killing the ones living in them because they are preserved with formaldehyde (HCHO) chemical compound; you know, the stuff that snakes and lizards were preserved in at school! Well, this is what they are breathing every day and, on top of that, the mold and mildew from the flood and dead bodies is going directly into their systems every day!

These people have no other place to go and "Uncle Sam" has billions of dollars lain away in reserve that they either give away or leave gathering dust! They say they have done what was best, but they have not done what is best!

Those little tin and vine-covered sticks called houses, what in the world will become of them in another class two hurricane? They'll never stand up. You know, I know, the people whose lives are at stake know it, and the most hateful rationalization is that our government knows it! It's almost as if they are waiting for some natural disaster to alleviate some of the over-population problem . . . or maybe there is oil under the Gulf they need more than human life!

These days, these "Dimes" . . . I know that money is not the root of all evil! Though I do know that the love of the stuff is. When and where do we draw the line? When is money not going to be more important than the lives of our fellow men?

If you're doing something that is going to equate the loss of another human with the money you receive, maybe it would be better to just stop! If selling a dime bag to a preteen means he will O.D., or if it means her life will end with her throat cut on some back alley street living the life of a hooker to feed her needle! Mr. or Ms., you need to eject yourself form the human race because you ain't human . . . you're a predator—a cannibal feeding on the flesh of your people! We don't need you, not in the least! You, my friend, are a rope, a knife, a gun. The stuff you sell is an illegal, lethal injection, and our people die not even being heard by a jury of twelve of their peers! You are the beast, anti-Christ, venom, snake!

This essay is not about Judgment. It is, however, about observation and I have observed the same processes of failure generation after generation! They call this generation: "Generation X!" I do not believe that this is anymore than a way to sabotage the minds of the young and the old so they will give up and stop trying even before they start! Generation X does not, has not, nor will it ever exist as long as God is on His seat in heaven and as long as we keep seeing beyond the wall that society has placed around these and those public housing constructs for the poor to be born, to live, to grow, and die in! You know, "out of sight, out of mind!" I've been out of my mind for several decades. People hear me all the time and "Anna" (for lack of a better name) "Polly-Anna" is consistently talking, criticizing, and accusing me of something!

"Anna" talks to you all as if she were your best friend and confidant. She could really care less about anyone! Her agenda is her own and is all about her and what "she" can get . . . get out of you for herself! Good ole "Polly want a cracker 'Anna'"! A talking parrot doesn't have a chance with "Anna" . . . her mouth is the gateway to hell!

At this juncture, you may have just laughed to yourself—it's not only because it may be an amusing statement but, more importantly, you know exactly what I'm talking about! You may even know of whom I'm talkin' about!

The moon is rising just over the horizon—one of those we don't see very often. It is enormous and red and full! The moon is full of blood. I wonder, "Is this what the Bible speaks of as a sign of the time of the end of time and life?"

I never let the end of life or time bother me. Albeit, it does every time I hear the cry of a baby, no matter the race. Children, to me, are so very precious and I don't think there will just be adults on Judgment Day . . . if you believe in such. Know what? I don't think they're all going to be old farts either; but a myriad of humankind, bumping and butting into each other for lack of livable space!

Mankind projects himself as seeing a perfect life and a perfect existence, even if we are killing one another in war after war.

Can we stop? Is it possible just maybe there's a chance for the "man" creature? He can devise almost any devil he wants to do his work, why can't he create peace among mankind? What is it that makes this striving beast called "man" so determined to live and yet so determined to kill each other, thereby annihilating self? Are we confused? Have we lost sight of a savior?

The star light has been seen beyond the fog-filled valleys below, a backdrop of blackness set in the heavens has given way to a bright sun shiny day!

Yet we all cannot see the clear blue skies through our brown and tearful eyes. And until we do, it is an obligation for all of us to put our hands to the plow, not looking back. For it is said that, "Any man who puts his hand to the plow looking back is not fit for the kingdom!"

We are "Kingdom Kids," all of us, not one to be left behind. If we will just get ourselves together and work as one, we will overcome all adversity, all harm!

The fight we must recognize is not amongst ourselves; and we need to stop anything—that is doing anything—that will hinder our forward advancement and our upward ascension! For the fight is against systems that have been set in place for eons to stop the children of God. We must above all things remember, "The battle is not given to the strong, nor the race to the swift, but to those that endure to the end!"

In order for us to endure, we must reckon our "old people" how they came through; how they suffered every indignation, yet their push coalition brought them forward because they never forgot who and whose they were!

Indeed, another man's trash can be the treasure of another.

I began *The Days of the Three Dimes* this morning with no small degree of apprehension. But I prayed and I know over years of ups and downs—doing with and doing without—that prayer can and does change things! I've seen times traveling along a dark, foggy, and cold road, no place to stop and rest, just having to push on, and out of no where a light shining through a stained glass window . . . a church! I have walked up to that church, bright and brand new it was, no one inside, but the doors just happened to be unlocked. I thank God and pray there. Then I take my pack for a pillow and lie down on the floor that smelled like fresh new wood, to fall into an angelic God-blessed sleep! Many such things have happened to me.

I'm neither saint nor too far gone sinner, but have counted my faith for righteousness and He rewards me daily . . . why not you?

This writ was not about everybody and his or her dog; but I tried to encapsulate the Black and why our blackness is important. Black men, for God's sake, don't feel left out; but the time has come to step up to the plate and give our ladies what they are really due! We got some fine women folk—and I don't just mean this by looking at them from behind, but looking at their overall carry! These females are the max. You know it, I know it, and every Tom, Dick, and Hairy Beast knows it. They deserve their accolades!

It was not to put them on a pedestal, for they are human and they have their failings, too! Yet when I look from Africa to Montezuma Pill Box Hills, these women stand tall!

This is a hard saying, but on the street even—and it should not be so—the Black prostitute has a respectable favor among her peers! Wherever me and you find her, she commands respect!

It hurts me to see her with her hair nappy and dirty clothes, filthy feet and sleep in the corner of her eyes, her teeth falling out or are knocked out by one of our so-called men!

They need someone to care . . . just care for them. To open your heart and hold this dirty, probably lousy, bug-covered creature in their arms and say, "No matter, baby, no matter. You are beautiful to me!" Because the obese and the crippled and the diseased are all products of a warped social order that have made them spare change; and they are golden bars and they need to know that . . . they really, really do!

The book of the "Dimes" has all the ingredients of life, some superimposed on these pages as if you were reading a novel. However, this simple man's essay of life in the Black Lane is neither novel, biography, history, or science. Although I think it acts as a lexicon of experiences of the Black culture in and of its bolstering itself up, yet it does not deny the failing points of the race and even gives some pointers on how we may at last truly overcome!

The Black race is not, was not, nor ever will it be the whipping boy or girl for the world cultures. But we will become just that if we do not take a stand and show the world our universal capabilities as men and women!

When it comes to intellect, the man is not short-changed. When it comes to him having a chance in every arena of life, he is. Therefore, it's time—and we are hard pressed for it—to make our own places and create our own chances, despite the government and the laws that cower us behind these social walls of bias!

Even in housing we are strategically placed behind an invisible barrier—a wall, if you will—and the oddity of it all is that our "phantasm" is self-produced. This phantasm magoria has kept us batting at the wind for so long until we think it is a normal part of life!

They give us illusions of grandeur or failure and neither is real. But to mind, they seem concrete enough to stop us from reaching into reality, grabbing the gold ring, and stepping as high as humanly possibly; finding ourselves instead of others at the top, thereby giving us something to pride in and point at as our successes!

We should be like ticks on a hound dog's back. We should be found in the greatest multiplicity in every endeavor and social order of this society. God only knows we've been here long enough to do so!

We know the society. We know its failing and we know it's successes. We know it well enough to gripe about how it has failed us. If then we have been watching how it is crumbling, then we know it well enough to change it and use it for our needs!

To just sit and point to the President and speak about how we believe he has failed is not enough. Everyone is speaking about how we believe he has failed America as a whole, so we are not alone!

The thing is, we as Black people have but for a few presidents (of which we can count on one hand) has failed the Black. Come on, when are we going to figure it out?!

First of all, we are a displaced people and this is not our homeland, even though we have been here for three hundred years. This really is not our home. It is thrown in our faces every time the chance arises. You know this is of a truth; but since we are here, not on a land where we have been for thousands of years, it is time to do as they say, "When in Rome, do as the Romans do!"

We're in America and there really are no people that indigenously belong here except the American Indian; and in truth, that is all! Everybody else is a transplant, but we are the only ones here against their will. We were perfectly happy right where we were in Africa!

America is truly the melting pot of human culture. But even in a melting pot, there is something called "sludge" or more a word that is not normally used as "slag!" This is what is left over after metal in its raw state is heated to its melting point. All the good stuff is blended together and the "slag" is what is left over and thrown away! If it came down to some kind of war or dissimulation of the races, and some race had to be left behind, we would be "slag!"

The truth is the light: let it shine on us, that knowing the undiluted truth, "it will make us free!"

We have worked hard in this culture. We have advanced this culture. But what part of the culture is more underpaid or underprivileged than the Black man?

There are councils that convene privy to our knowledge and talk about they will do with the Black if the choosing ever arise! As much as we have contributed to this society, these things even here in the new millennium take place!

It would seem with us marrying and openly dating our posture in the entertainment field and even in government, this would not be so!

I fear that we are not just entertainers but "entertainment" in the foulest form of the word—as a small mouse is entertainment for a cat just before the thing bites its head off!

This may or may not come as some kind of surprise to you depending on how well you are paid or your supposed social posture or platform. For those well-to-do, the illusion is grandest and they keep climbing. And they don't look back until they hit that well-placed ceiling; and they realize they were just being fooled and had allowed themselves to fool themselves into thinking, "Life is good." Then one day some little nondescript let's you have it right in the face with that infamous word and you realize you are still "Black!"

It's not that we are so insignificant because God only knows that without our sheer will and raw muscle, this country would not have had the push to be where it is now! The American Rail of Progress was lain primarily by the muscle and will of the Black man!

When the American-Indian War was fought, one of the finest riflemen was the Black man. And every war that has been fought for this country's beliefs and freedoms, the Black man many times either was in or led the charge. He has picked wounded white men up who were threatened of death on their backs, carried them for miles, and saved their lives. Yet when they came back to the country they had fought, bled, and, yes, died for, they could not sit on a stool and eat with other human beings. Everyone was accepted but the Black man!

"Past . . . we know the past," you may say. Yet as far as we have advanced as a society and a culture living in this society, we are still left behind! "What can we do?" I'll ask the question again. I pose this answer: We need to educate our children in the public sector and the private homes of the Afro-American. From the cradle to the grave, we need to educate, educate, educate! We need to make ourselves an indispensable commodity, one the whole world can't do without! Don't place ourselves in a position of a "bargain basement buy!" Place ourselves in a position that we can bargain with success for our success! You know how they fight over our athletes and pay them astronomical figures of money? Every Black man should have the same worth! Do you know why they can call their own numbers?

It's because they make the betting world fat with dollars every time they play! The entertainment world is run and succeeds because the actor or singer (or whatever he or she does) makes the public and private sector fat, fat, fat! You may be surprised to realize that the stock exchange moves according to the way these kind of Blacks function—not alone, mind you; but they play a very significant role therein!

If it were not that we were so numerous, we would become just that! Yet don't lean or sit on our laurels thinking that we don't have anything to worry about because one thing is certain: a sweeping, well-placed, genetically-coded disease could wipe us all out in one year! I do believe that there are those that know of cures for Aids and HIV and cancer but won't give that cure because it is more economically sound to let people die! There are more Blacks catching cancer and dying than ever in our history; and Aids, everyone knows is at epidemic proportions!

They spend more money (that is, our government) on a hundred bombs than they do on any form of disease research like Aids! Why? Because they would rather kill than to promote life; and as you look at the world population, you can almost see why!

This day is a day where by some standards we all as humanity cross our fingers, have our four-leaf clovers, hedge our bits on our stock, keep garlic over the door, or some other magical totem to ward off evil! I looked and I did not have two nickels to rub together, but I did have "three dimes" laying in a perfect vertical line along the edge of a beat-up bureau that I am determined to never spend!

A totem? I don't know! An encouragement of this I am sure!

This book takes some punches at some many devils, not a people, a demon of demons. It was not meant to be burdensome. That's why you can find a light-hearted affair with life herein!

We as a people were not meant, I believe, by God to be the buttock of society nor the laughing stock nor the whipping boy or girl or men or women! We are a proud, beautiful, wonderful, spicy people full of culture and lore. Our contact along life's labored path has caused us to come in contact with every culture on the earth and, instead of us becoming like them, we have maintained self! Therein more than enough to be proud of!!

We dance to their music, but they imitate our own. Everything on this earth can feel the lunge of the Black man's thrust! He is powerful. And not only should we stand as great bed mates, but we are powerful people or we would not, could not have lasted for so long!

We have watched cultures and societies one behind the other rise and fall, decimated and even totally annihilated by cold-blooded war and murder . . . yet we stand!

In Antebellum, we scurried for cover from the slaver's lash . . . but we stand. We were given the white man's trash called "religion" and we found God! We were starved in post-World War II . . . we survived. We and many whites froze in Korea . . . we don't get much thanks, yet we stand! Pearl Harbor, many planes were brought down by a Black cook that manned the guns! Praised—yes; dead—yes; but his people have not the glory they have over the years conceptualized. Yes, we live better, some of us; but what happened to our (for every Black born) that "40 acres and that mule?" Not just the acreage, but every promise this government and this people promised us? What happened to it?

This book is not like my first book . . . that people are afraid to read and pretend they don't know exists! It does not have profanity in it that describes the hell and horror of one man's suffering along with many more in this nation; but it is full of dirty deeds that are handed to the Black man and are expected for him to consume without request or compromise.

It was not meant to be a dirty book; neither was *AT THE CRSS*. It, like *AT THE CRSS*, tells some hard truth!

This book, *The Days of the Three Dimes* is a "lavage"—the therapeutic washing out of an organism; in this case, the Black culture! We need to stop dancing for just a little while!

I would like to quote a poet at this point because this person is a master and I want to honor, as well as lift a word, their words!

I quote "First Fight. Then Fiddle" by Gwendolyn Brooks:
First fight. Then Fiddle. Ply the slipping string
With feathery sorcery; muzzle the note

<end excerpting>

Again, this is not my writ, not my poetry, but the poetry of Ms. Gwendolyn Brooks.

This poem epitomizes my effort and the effort of these "Dimes." Ah! These "Dimes." It's not fair to those that came before us, fought, lived, died in the effort to secure our freedom! It's not wrong to dance and to sing, and to tell a Black this is to rage war with his soul, mind, and spirit; for we are a harmonious people. We make the music that we and others can't help but dance to!

Yet like Gwendolyn Brooks' poem "First Fight. Then Fiddle," it tells of a time hidden within the stanzas when the Black was threatened by horrible atrocities. It warned and reminded us!

To me it says, "Don't get too comfortable." For as America rages war on over the world to sustain a kind fleeting "moth to the candle flame" peace, we as suffered souls under the fist of the same tyrant must realize the blow, that crushing blow, is never that far away!

We must take time to teach our young ones of all the times that we were treated treacherously and abandoned by a country that have had to slave for, work underpaid, our living conditions that for the mass has not changed much in a hundred years! How they expect more and more of us; at the same time allowing us to have and make less and less.

I hear the moaning and the groaning from the peanut gallery, as if the words I write were a lie. You know the general consensus is "that all of that and this is unnecessary." Do you know why we stay in this stagnant state? Well it's because of the general consensus.

The government has trained us that it is better to have peace and not think along these lines and we, "we don't want no trouble!" Sorry; sound check, "one, two!" We got trouble for as long as we are first class contributors to a system that would be crushed without our labor and our ability to handle a weapon of warfare and treated like third and fourth and last class citizens . . . we got trouble!

Now I may sound like a retro-age "Black Panther" to some degree; but in actuality, I am a humble minister/evangelist walking along a well-worn trail, marked by chained and shuffling feet. The oddity, some don't even wear physical chains, but indeed are chained by social mores that society has clasped around our feet and dare us to remove!

We will never be free until we become strong enough to demand every ounce of our freedom, no matter the sacrifice. As a people, the only way we can ever do this is by holding on to a true relationship with God our "Savior," not our "Master," but indeed a "Teacher Superlative," and let go of the superstitions of the past!

We must first learn to trust one another. But before we can do that, we must give each other a reason for trust. I believe this concept is imbedded in our fundamental praise, our relationship with our teacher. We must hope that the teacher teaches the same thing as the Superlative Teacher, and no less will do!

I've found that all teachers on the superlative level teach always the same super-substantial teaching. In other words, their thoughts are very concrete and can be traced from one teacher to the next. This is so because ultimately there is only one truth, one guideline—from Buddha to Christ to Mohammed to Brahman—all teach the construct that "we search for the truth and it will make us free!"

Now me, I'm a Southern Missionary Baptist Evangelist/Minister. Though I am, I am not prejudice and I feel that every religious persuasion has its degree of savvy based in truth. You have to not go blindly along in any of the persuasions!

It's all right to choose what you will believe, but be sure by much examination that what you believe is "Der Truth!"

How can you tell the truth from myth or an out-and-out lie? This is a basic and simple process: compare what you know from station to station. The truth is concise, complete, and congruous. It conserves and preserves and always serves life. Consider this and your eyes will open.

I know at first the light will be so scintillating that it would threaten to blind! Dare look anyway. If you will, the light will dismiss every shackle and you will be free! I know you are wondering at this moment, "Well, scribe, what do you believe?" The question should be more aptly put, "In what religion do you believe?"

Now here comes the "rub." I don't believe in any "rubbish" and the religion must exemplify "truth!" You tell me what religion I believe in!

Religion is the ice cream cone without the ice cream. Tastes good, but it leaves you a "lackey" (foot man, flunky, a servile follower, toady, hanger on): these lackey, lacking yes!

Now the striving beast is upon the "grassy noetic knoll." His striving with me has stopped. I sit calmly surveying forever. I see all the races of man flowing like a great ocean lapping almost sleepily at the sandy shores of time!

For every grain of sand that is pulled into the salty surf, a birth; and for every birth a death! While the erosion of the earth by life goes on systematically and continuously while God looks on!

Intellectual man seems drawn further and further away from Him as He continues to hold to our infantile hand as we search more and more through the mysteries of the world and space that we live on and in.

The beast has stopped wheezing air and his nostrils work normally. There is no more smoke or flames pouring forth from them.

Maybe in my fear of the night the fog and the cold even of the thrashing ride, flames were easy to see and his black flanks seem to be carrying me into the very bowels of hell . . . the unknown will do that to a being!

I know this creature is not tame nor timid, but proud and strong; yet it has stopped and has allowed me to envision this glorious sight of mankind in his passing.

Neither heaven nor hell frights me from this vantage point. And life is where it stands and I stand where life is; as I've dismounted and take time to be humble in a world so full of extraordinary wonders so full of joy and song!

Even bereavement has its place now and it must be for a time. For death is the twin sister of life. Different by no means, for by it we gained the right to live!

There is one Superlative Teacher I watch each day. He bore the cross for another superlative after He had fell to His knees and was crushed under the wait of the burden of wood and all the sins of men!

If you believe in such things!?

He, too, was whipped with the lash called the "whip" known now as the cat of "nine tails." He, too, felt the wait of the cross and, like the great sacrifice, had done on that day no wrong. One called "Niger," Simeon was his name and "Black" bore the cross the rest of the way to Golgotha's Hill, that mount called "The Skull!"

Maybe this is why we as Black men and women are given such "curses" tied together in a bundle with such "blessing!" We as a people are the most blessed and simultaneously cursed almost in the same breath!

Maybe this is the reason some one coined the phrase, "The first prayer ends in the last curse!"

But God says draw nigh unto me and I will draw nigh unto you. I feel that a God that is the author and finisher of a blessing like faith must bring His blessing with Him! While the author of perfect praise must draw down the ear of Him that is being praised, while "wash-shup" is going on, I believe God comes a little bit closer and brings His blessing with His spirit! In the spirit of joy the curse is lifted and forgotten and all we see is his glorious appearing!

In this ride, I've found life to be exhilarating, fearful, joyous; even though through excruciation of life I've found the truth and I know that truth has set me free! No! Made me free!

For you must understand giving this I have not tried to cram any kind or my kind of religion down your throat—for lack of a better word. I've left open doors behind me during the ride. It was so speedy and so brisk I had not the time to explore the rooms that they opened unto!

I left signs all along the way floating in the steam that was flowing from my mouth out onto the cold night and sea air; this mist is your guidepost!

Without argument, I left you very little to grasp. The one mile stone that is and will always be is the common denominator—our exile!

By and only by proximity can we claim America. And this not a literal psychogenic. It holds a certain and very certain truth. It lays outside the sphere of physical science or knowledge but claims our spirit as its own!

I don't want to gripe about the same thing, but fat meat has no certain taste! Eat and die. But give the prophet his cake as the widow did "Elijah": her meal barrel never being empty and her cruise of oil always full where empty before was!

How can we relate to what we as many an intellectual, the highly intelligent calls "myth"? Things that don't happen today and many teachers don't teach. How can we relate to an unknown?

Atoms make up everything known to man, but observe a single atom by the human eyes and none other method has never been done. Now we find that science has discovered a thing called a "double negative particle" existing within the atom. Before that they found something else they did not know existed in the atom. It was called the "neutron." Oddly given the most advance mechanism, neither can be seen, only experienced. But the gravity of their existence is so weighty that their place in the atom to say they do not exist would be to deny the existence of the atom itself, thus to deny that we as beings and being itself is only a wispy dream possibly dreamed by God who cannot be seen either.

"What are you—agnostic, atheist, believer? Scribe, you know what I am!" I may very well know what you are, but I also know what God is.

I stand at the base of Kilimanjaro (Kilimanjaro is the great mountain found in Africa). I stand with my nose pressed tight at its base structure and I can't see the whole mountain. Reader, can you see the whole reasoning?

I'm not trying to be evasive, but God after all is said to have made all that we know. It is also said that He sits above everything and all that we are and know are at His feet. Is He clothed in a long white robe? No, He's wrapped in darkness and the seas are His foot paths! The ocean and seas of the earth? No, the eternal oceans and seas of eternity! Does He have a long white beard? No, He is not Grandfather Time! He is the Maker and Creator of time and the Father of all things. Does He have lightening bolts in His hands to strike down any sinner for any of his least sins? No, God is a spirit though as real as a double negative! Knowing that the double negative exists in nature, there is always a complementary force! Conversely speaking, there must be a double positive! If that is so, that, if anything, I would call God would be it! For God is good. How do you know God is good? Everything in creation is as it should be for nothing is out of kilter. Even the greatest storm and earthquake, volcanoes are a must and in its place! We see it as horror because human life is lost and we are able to see the destruction today even as it happens making it even more horrible. But at the same time, men are becoming anesthetized to horror. The more we see, the less it affects! Man seems to be adjusting to great catastrophic events in his world, in that he feels helpless before it!

War and rumors of wars, man has died always ever since he was born and has borne sin on his back! If you believe in such things?!

God is not an avenging devil that takes our loved ones away from us! He neither is an angel of perfect world without hazard.

He put existence into motion and, as a perfect working perpetual machine, everything functions right on time! O yes, we can cause great calamity in our world merely by our actions—whether it be thoughts or physical activities, positive or negative—we play a very definite role in how human life will move!

Example: we pollute the river, the silt stops up the fish's gills, it can't breath, it dies, the creatures that feed on the fish have nothing to eat, they starve, they die, the seeds that are carried in the bird dung that reseeds the field and the forest are no longer present, the forest starts to dwindle, the atmosphere is affected because the oxygen is decreased, the forest starts to dwindle and die, the bear that feeds in the forest has no place to live, man's air is being polluted, he can't breath as well as he did, his lungs are affected and infected, he takes drugs to overcome the affect of despairing lungs, the drugs have not been tested well enough, the drugs give us cancer, we die!

Why then do we blame God who created a perfect perpetual machine when we have stuck our fingers in the works and thumbed our nose at Him?

We will die. We always have. It's the twin sister of life!

"Scribe, now dog-gone-it, what is God anyhow? Where is He? I've looked and I can't see Him anywhere."

All I can answer is with a question: How close is your nose to the mountain?

You see, in order to see God, we have to look at the whole of what we see! Stop taking atoms apart and stand and look up at a sequoia, glance into the eyes of a baby—I don't care whether brown or blue, you'll see the same thing!

Start counting the stars in heaven and when you can't, let your eyes settle on the brightest one that you choose. You'll see they all sing the same song!

Follow the rise and fall of a mountain range. Catch a snowflake; watch it melt in your hand then catch one on your tongue and enjoy that snow. No other flavor flake that we all know!

We're not so much different. It's just the fear of the unknown that makes us afraid!

Greed does not even have the kill power as the unknown! We see a bug we've never seen before. The first thing we do is squash it!

We're not that much different. In truth, we're a lot the same! But what about your skin? Black, you mean? The earth is black and so are the heavens. Are they any less beautiful?

Enough, enough with the prose. Give me something I can feel!

Okay. Feel this! You are beautiful like nothing I've ever seen, nothing at all! You exist and the depth of what you are has never been measured!

I can't touch you, nor can you touch me. Like a seraph to me, I see you like looking through a pane of the clearest most polished glass!

Your place in the world is but a hand breath from the depths of the deepest darkest ocean that no one has ever seen. And you are so pure until, when you are placed against the backdrop of a snow bank, you become invisible. To me your place I cannot enter. And my home you only see from the outside!

You don't know me and your will is like a whisper in my head, like a breeze that passes and shakes the daffodil then is gone and I can't follow it home!

You appear and disappear like a card in a magician's hands. And like the cutting act of the same human body once whole, you are in a twinkling of an eye half!

A spring you are up out of the ground, no direction to show from whence you came; then into the ground again!

You're a watcher and keeper of a place called earth that came into being by the will of God.

Time you control with day light and spring forward, then fall back.

Buttes you stand upon while astraddle your dirt bikes and the land cries, "No more, please no more!"

Can you feel me? Huh? Can you feel me?!

What we are is the human race. And if we don't stop so much racing, we won't have a track to race upon!

Can you feel me, ladies, gentlemen?

It's now 12:13 AM midnight and I have become like as unto the striving beast. Matter of fact, we as the Indians were with their ponies when they rode, they and the earth were as one!

The date is September the 2nd, 2007, Sunday morning . . . The Sabbath, if you believe in such!

I end as I started yesterday . . .

Dear God,

Forgive me of my sins. Bless mankind and my kin. Deliver all of the sick and shut-ins. Let the dead some day rise again!

Change the eternal course of man. Place your blessing upon this land and upon our children who fight and protect in lands far and near.

Remove the prejudice and the fear. Lord God, wipe every tear!

Deliver the man behind prison bars. Shut the door between sickness and death from someone and eventually every one who upon their beds do lay!

Tender hands, I implore for my little grands and the grands of every grandfather and grandmother, no matter their skin, across this world and across this land!

Don't judge me, O Lord, too harshly, for the pangs I let pour. I know my mouth can leave a gaping sore; but peace I seek here not war!

As time ticks along, my age is ever increasing and death winks at me in his passing. I just pray that I will have deserved you being there when on life I shut the door!

Peace is the pleasure of not knowing nightmares in the daytime, and I pray for the mentally ill that they won't have chains on body or mind!

Dear, dear Father, treat the war leaders as they lay upon their beds let them have horrible dreams that curse their head. Let them see every shade of every warrior that died at their command and let them mend their ways, and let their raised hand to attack be stayed.

Lord, thank you for dying for men and, just to let you know, I believe in such as this—the time, the place, the test!

Give, O God, to the hungry and homeless, the destitute, a place to lay their head tonight; and when the morning comes, a place to get a bite!

I know, Lord, you can do all things and do all things well. Let not the hurricane too many and the oceans swell!

Lord, I pray for the Katrina victims who are still victims, victims now to the bureaucracy!

As I sit and do pray and upon these pages these lines and words do say, I pray you will draw nigh to anyone that calls on you this Sabbath day in true repentance and request. At this point, I will take a rest!

But, Lord, I must say and ask a few more things. For my sister I cry and sing, wash over her body and with your healing hand dismiss any and all of her sickness!

My nieces, nephews, great and small, please, dear God, bless them all. And my great aunts and my wife's kin, too, sister-in-laws, brother-in-laws, forgive me, Lord, but I'll soon be through.

The leaders of this world—white, yellow, brown, and white/Black and Black, too—though I know they are said to be some of the shades of the rainbow, but in truth for the Black I've never seen any come into sight.

For the life of me the white man is pinto, the Indian is copper, the brown man is brown, the Asiatic is tawny or light beige, never any other do I know . . . Praise the Lord a green man, we're through.

Now Lord, betwixt you and I, there's but little to say. Bless you from the crown on your head to the soles of your feet.

The Holy Spirit, the Son, Most High—may peace dwell between you and I.

Forever these things I pray you will adjust my life to accommodate, Lord, keep food upon mine and my family's plates!

Clothes on my back, shoes on our feet; though I know I don't have to ask for these needs—you always meet!

Now Lord, bless the unblessed and somehow bless the ones that cursed and can't be blessed. I don't believe that any is too far from your touch, not one, not even the blasphemer—he's a fool, but you made him, too!

Remember, O God, your Son died for all and all the sins of all men!

I'm almost done, O Lord, be cause I know if I keep doing this, I'll soon see the Son!

The day is gone, the night is far spent. I need, dear God, and all these words a man child truly meant!

There is nothing too great for you for you can accomplish all and anything will pass until all has come to pass!

I'm tired but I want to thank you for giving me a chance. Now if I could have just one tiny glance at one twinkle in one of your eyes beautiful; this before I leave Mother Earth I would like to see.

Lord, I feel the burden of the natural world more and more each day. And to the demon at my door I will say, "In the name of Jesus Christ be struck dumb and until your mouth opens to speak in this way, do you stay!"

Teach me, teach me, O Lord, to sing a proper praise and to teach the world of you every day. Give me this right and this chance to do pray.

Or have you answered before I can ask? These words already written in eternity, I the sounding brass!

Bless my church and the great chapel I am yet to see. Bless, O God, out of eternity!

Herein, O Lord, is my humble prayer. From me to you as always the word of agreement: Amen!

Sleep is upon me now and this beast stands upon its feet and sleeps.

The tools of the scribe are becoming laborious and the one o'clock hour is upon us for the most we sleep!

The Days of the Three Dimes draws nigh. It's close and I can only hope and pray to God . . . God, I do pray that many a thousand will read and hereby grow toward one another, upward toward you and away from sin!

It would seem that the ride is an addictive thing with all its pain, horrors, beauty, and dreams. I don't want to think that each one that rides eventually cries out to the striving beast, "Don't stop, don't ever stop!"

Yet knowing this it is not the pain of an unaccustomed rider that hurts so much. It is the knowledge that one must need to stop somewhere along the road and leave the creature with the creator for someone else to experience, for someone else to ride.

The striving beast is not meant for just one, but each mother's child that parts the legs in birth must someday ride alone! His experience the same, but completely different from any rider before!

This *The Days of the Three Dimes*—these the days that God has given each of us alone and together! We as humanity must learn how to live life, enjoy life, and to try and understand the things that were never meant for man to perceive in the first place!

I feel that after watching me through these lines, you are amazed that one such as I can pray! Well, what did you expect an old scribe to do after walking with God all life long? There is but little else I would do. He's been my light in a blinded world. He's been my joy in a world filled with tears, remorse, and frustration!

I won't ask you to forgive me of but one thing: and that is I had to string you to keep you so that by chance Satan gets in your way, you won't succumb and fall away! I would not have any to be lost!

Last but not least, I am in no wise prejudice, except for needless wrongs from one man to another! The Black people are my people, so are the Cherokee, but I love all mankind! I can't look at a little child's face—no matter whose child it is—and hate it!

Albeit, I know there are men and women who desperately hate our children—not adults—babes. For this reason, I've sat down with an ink pen in my hand and have written many things that I see (mainly to my people) as a warning and to all that read this writ. Reckon your world and the part you play in its survival, and know that the way you treat other men is a major player in how they will treat you; and how you treat one another will determine the outcome of our natural world!

Jesus the Christ said, "Choose life, not death!" He is the master of wisdom and the word incarnate!

Let's look at one other concept . . .

I know even as a Black that the world has evolved in such a way until privacy is almost impossible. We pretend while being nosey about other people's business! Yet we can't as a nation perceive when a man mad will attack and kill scores as Cho did. (I spoke on him and a few more at the beginning of the writing.) We can't perceive where Bin Laden is hiding or even if he is alive. We can't pray with other churches, synagogues, and/or temples; yet we know what goes on across town! Our world is upside down and topsy-turvy. We wait and depend on the "legal mafia" to relieve us of our troubles, and all the government will do is charge us higher and higher costs for just about everything!

Listen, don't stop your eyes or ears now. It's very important that we face up and fess up to our problems! I like honesty. I don't like lying or liars. Get my drift?

Stop thinking well it's kind of like riding the striving beast. Once you start, you can't stop; and once the beast starts to stop on it's own, you don't want the ride to end.

Yet there is one thing we can do. It's called "good old common sense courtesy!"

I don't know what's going on I anyone's house but my own, and I don't want to! This is how it has always been for me since the inception of extra-normal knowledge. I just chose to stick around my own bed and I've done so forever; at least the forever of my tiny life!

The problem does not arise with knowing; it comes in red with bulging eyeballs and veined heads of lust, arrogance, greed, prejudice, disrespect, and hate!

Now as I've said before, "I ain't mad at cha'!" Just stay out of my way and my ink pen and you'll be all right!

You know what they say, "A petition well placed with enough signatures on it can change the position of the house!" "The pen is mightier than the sword!"

I've been openly behind my back accused of messing with people's heads. Now how can I mess with people's heads? Just tell me. Now come on, who am I? I'm just a country boy with a little . . . . education.

Brevity is good for the soul and it's 1:59 AM I've at this almost all afternoon and evening and night of yesterday!

With nothing more than a pen—well a few pens in that they soon run ink dry—I've written this essay! Hope you enjoy reading it as much as I did writing it!

The Days of the Three Dimes is five pages from success. I will have finished my third book and I have done them all in one year!

Not that this is part of the writing as such, but if you read herein maybe you can appreciate the task and the torment of handwriting a manuscript here in this modern day with PCs and word processors and all of that gadgetry. I guess I just like to sweat, get funky, and get right down on my knees with my work!

I don't know if this will make you dig deep, but I hope so. O, I don't mean in your wallet or pocketbook! Matter of fact, you can borrow someone else's copy to read. "If you dig my jive," "if you feel me," "if you can connect with my head," maybe you already have!

Hum! Heck, that may reduce sells!

When I say things like that, you can believe I'm getting punch happy and need my medicine! "Medicine?" you ask. Yes, medicine. I have PTSD. I am a Vietnam veteran and I'm mighty proud of it—medicine or no!

I really and truly believe that there are many persons along the Gulf Coast who were Katrina victims who are silently and alone considering suicide because they keep thinking the same thoughts over and over; not just any thoughts—thoughts of the horror of those weeks—and that, my friend, is what PTSD really is!

You're not mad. You're overwhelmed by the sheer weight of the stress of the experience! The sad thing is they don't have doctors tending them. They should, but don't. They need medicine. They need homes. They need money, laws, and lawyers that will protect them from thugs that take their lives—physically and mentally and socially! They need aid beyond FEMA trailers—that, by the way, are killing them—and they need protection from another impending hurricane disaster! They need the government not giving enough and the people of these great United States should! That's all there is to that! We just should. These are Americans just down the road!

It's not as though they were a third world country "out of sight, out of mind"—though we should belly up to the bar and help them, too! I know, it's easier . . . .

Well you now know my pet peeves—it is suffering humanity—and I know I can't save the world by myself or overnight; but together we as a people could!

Now is the time to say, "I will." And I will myself take an active part in making my house, my neighborhood, my town or city, my country, this world a better and safer place for all mankind! If it's ever going to get done, we can't depend on the governments to do it; because it is monetarily beneficial for war, havoc, and mayhem to continue and at an escalating pace!

America is a great country but as of late it is failing so many of its own—outright and seemingly without shame!

The Black almost began to expect to be neglected; but now everybody but cheap labor is being neglected!

"Give me liberty or give me death!" It kind of looks like the government would rather give us death! I may be wrong, I'm just a scribe; I write what I see is wrong.

Who died and made me the <u>conscience</u> of the world? Well no one did! The conscience I use is my own! When I see people, human beings, die needlessly out of social and governmental neglect, I don't know about you, but my conscience is pricked and my heart bleeds because of it!

Why the days of the "Dimes" came to be this kind of statement, I do not know. Maybe God intended it to be this way from the very beginning. When I started this book, it was never in this vein. But they say novels take on their own spirit; but no one said anything bout an essay!

I don't regret having come down this path. It's been a little scary, but I have a rewarder of them that diligently seek Him!

I can't say that I am on some kind of conscious pilgrimage toward God each day because I'm not; and I make mistakes—lots of them! Albeit, I've found that it's not how many times you fall, but eventually you're judged for how many times you get up!

I guess working and knowing any degree of law makes you, to some degree, a degree of "pig!" They say you are what you eat, and I love chicken; so I guess since I am a male I could be considered a cockerel—not just a rooster, mind you, but a rooster with a razor! A fighting cock! A whole different ball of wax!

It's 3:00 AM the next day and, as you can read, I'm still writing. I've just got to finish this now! These "Dimes" have been a task for me, but I believe I enjoyed the work! If you're reading this, then you're reading me . . . one way or another, you're reading me!

Out of all I can or could say to you is whether you are of some religious affiliation, agnostic, or atheist, you need to reconsider your stance. You know, we make mistakes sometimes—sometimes mighty big ones! It would be a horror and shame to miss heaven and end up in hell out of nothing more than stubbornness!

If you don't understand what's happening to you and you wonder why you ended up with this book in your hands, it just may be that somebody bigger than all of us sees you as very special and very important and doesn't want to let you destroy yourself. If this is plausible, pray. Just talk to God like you talk to your best friend or your worst enemy, no matter, just talk to Him. He'll do the rest! I can promise you that He will be moved! Slowly at first, even imperceptibly, but He will move!

Your enemy is O so beautiful satin, Satan! The one that hot butter won't melt on his tongue; the eternal liar. Strangely enough, he is most of our friend. Did you know the most mishaps and mistakes you get caught up in are caused by demons that despise man? They're not your friend. They are the enemy. Don't doubt and don't forget; for as soon as you forget it, you will find yourself right back in the pit you just ascended from! That's their job and they do it well!

Another sad thing is preachers and ministers don't preach or teach much about the dark side anymore. And they are quick to tell you, "Ah, you give the devil too much credit!" Or they'll say, "You can't blame the devil for everything; you have to take an account." But by saying this, they leave you hopeless and without any form of refuge out of the demonic storm that is raging in the world today.

I declare you can blame the devil! These are the lost days and Satan and his hordes know it. They are not sitting idly by but are gearing up for the final assault and the final battle!

Much lack and now concern in high ranking places is there because—you guessed it—ole slew foot is there leading the way to a downward spiral, with a promise that if we all say "yes" there's nothing God can do and hell will be heaven! Even this flimsy tell sounds like the brash roaring of the lion of Hades! He does exist and his greatest accomplishment would be to have you think he does not!

As a minister, I'm obligated to warn and prepare! There's a very real battle . . . no, war raging on the celestial shores and men are the chess pieces that are being used. Unlike conventional chess, even the pawns carry great weight and authority; that's why Satan never rests!

Sometimes I feel sorry for him never being able to rest. Not! I'm glad he can't rest in this present time nor ever in eternity!

It's 3:32 AM. Welcome to my world. This is the time when they are most active; this is the time you need to be prayed up, baby!

Because these are the hours when the psyche is most vulnerable, this is when his minions work the hardest—the witches, the Satanist, the black magician! Sounds arcane—well maybe. But these creatures do not recognize time as anything more than a good time or bad time to influence some unsuspecting wayfarer!

The Days of the Three Dimes—not time, not dance, nor is it even romance—but very basic truths that we all know and despise. Why? Because the truth is painful. But if you are ever to be free, you must find it, accept it, and even, yes, embrace the hot coals of it to your bosom! Only in this way will you burn away the mucous that fills the wounds in our heart; that the heat may staunch the wound and kill the bacteria of sin and/or wrong doing!

No dog that has been chained all its life wants to run away, even though the chain has been removed. He although will venture further and further away from his tether, until he is so far away from it, until he realizes his freedom and then the joy can be recognized—even in a dog.

What blows my mind is man—the intelligent beast—chooses and many times much prefers to be chained to his peg or his troubles rather than taking his two hands and removing merely by his own will the collar and chain from around his neck, thus being free!

Instead, as the "Dimes" close, we can see impertinent suckling at his wrongs and enjoying the bitter of his briny feast!

Eyes peering around, always checking to see if there is someone watching. It doesn't matter if the whole world watches, many of them are doing the same thing!

Look, O people, your redemption draweth nigh!

The Dimes.